Can't we All Just Get Along?

The Paul Dysart Story

By Paul E. Dysart, Sr.

Can't We All Just Get Along?

(c) copyright 2020 by Paul E. Dysart, Sr.
All rights reserved.

Cover Design: HenkinSchultz
Book Design: Kelli Schmidt-Bultena

Made in the USA

Introduction

As Paul often says, "Why can't we all just get along?"

Paul Dysart, Sr. has lived a life filled with experience, both complicated and colorful. The story begins with his family's move from an all-Black neighborhood in Kansas to a predominately white community in South Dakota. Sioux Falls, SD is where he recalls the many firsts that occurred for him: first Black family to attend as parishioners at Saint Joseph Cathedral and students at St. Joseph Cathedral School (1946), first Black man to work at John Morrell's (1964), the first Black Realtor in South Dakota (1978).

The story is also comprised of complicated family dynamics: affairs, divorce, prison and pardons. It is in the messy reality that one is able to uncover what is important — the lessons about welcoming family, voicing your truth and sharing love.

Throughout this book you'll find many possible life lessons from Paul's vast experiences. We've highlighted these bits of wisdom with a lightbulb at the top of those pages.

What follows is the story of Paul's life as inspired by the stories he shared with me from 2017 through 2020, along with the many pieces he has written and collected through the years.

Kelli Schmidt-Bultena

Ask for the Order

Because I didn't plan on living this long, I did a terrible job of setting up financial, end of life, and taking care of yourself money. Social Security does almost take care of a basic portion of your personal cost of living. However, as they say, if it is to be, it's up to me. With that in mind, at 80, not very mobile, in the midst of a Pandemic, and over 50 million people newly unemployed, the job market dictates to me that I write this book, and sell it alongside Dysart's Just Right BBQ and meat sauce. My personal memory of life in our beautiful country from 1940 to 2020 through these brown eyes and Black body with the help of my wordsmith Kelli Bultena, I put in a book that is an easy read. The meat sauce makes all types of meat more palatable as it has for our family as long as I can remember.

Rather than wait for someone else to say it, I want to express my appreciation to the people of the metro of Brandon, Harrisburg, and Tea, SD, Lincoln, Turner, and Minnehaha County's, especially Sioux Falls, South Dakota, for continually giving everyone the opportunity to fit in and improve their lot in life. From 1946 to the midst of the Pandemic, the vast overall mindset of the people in this region was "I'm here to help if needed'. I leave you with — Watch out, our quality of life has been exposed!!!

So please, stay safe, consider an old man's plea to purchase the book and a bottle of Just Right sauce and tell your family and friends.

Paul E. Dysart, Sr. (September 1, 2020)

Can't We All Just Get Along?
The Paul Dysart Story

The Move (1946) 6

Life Lessons (1958) 34

Settling Down (1962) 44

Making Changes (1976) 51

The Prison Experience (1982) 62

Building & Rebuilding a Family (ongoing) 71

Building a Business (1985) 76

Pardons (2003) 90

Dysart's Just Right BBQ Sauce 95

From Emmett Till to Black Lives Matter 97

Extras & Snapshots 101

Acknowledgments 127

The Move (1946)

Lettie held his small hand in hers as they stood at the train station. She felt the presence of Frances behind her, his quiet calm bringing a feeling of safety and security not often found in 1940's Kansas for a young Black woman. Their eyes met and they both smiled.

Lettie looked him over—Frances' blonde hair, blue eyes and that white clergy collar around his neck. She looked away, and then down at her young son.

Paul was only four years old, the third of her five children. The only one diagnosed with vitiligo; patches of white covered his small brown chest. Her doctor had said to stop the loss of color he needed shots. Once a week she and Paul left Atchison and took the train to Kansas City. Frances was by their side, bringing a piece of candy for Paul and peace of mind for Lettie. The trio would take the train and spend a night at a hotel in Kansas City.

As they boarded the train, Paul smiled happily, sandwiched between the two adults, the butterscotch candy tasting sweet in his mouth. He climbed up to sit on his mother's lap once the train was moving and watched as the trees began to zip by. The train station seemingly getting smaller and smaller as they went. When he could see it no longer, he turned back to study his momma's hand as she patted his leg. He traced the fine brown lines on her knuckles and he laughed when she pulled it away and told him to keep to himself. Frances smiled down at him.

Paul recalls spending time with Frances this way, thinking of him as the kind Catholic priest that brought candy to the kids. What unfolded in the years that followed was a story of intertwining lives, and lessons in love, amid complications.

It was 1946, Paul's father, Scoop (Lawrence A. Dysart) worked for Kerford Quarry Company, which became the catalyst for moving the family to South Dakota. Kerford Company opened a quarry in Sioux Falls, a predominantly white city in Southeast South Dakota. Scoop was recruited. He was about 30 years old at the time; he and his wife Lettie had five children. Scoop left the family behind in Kansas to determine if it would be a good move, and evidently he felt it was; just a few months later Lettie and the children made the move after him.

The Dysart family left Atchison and traveled 335 miles north. In 1946 the Sioux Falls population was 45,000 and about 150 of those folks were Black. Paul said it was a stark difference from the all Black neighborhood they moved from.

The Dysarts were a Catholic family. Coming to Sioux Falls, the Dysarts became the only Black family in St. Joseph's Cathedral — in the church, at the school and on the block. It wasn't something Paul thought about a lot, but his parents told him not to go south of Eighth Street.

Soon after the family settled into their Sioux Falls home, their old priest Frances came to see them, only now Frances had taken the collar off. Paul was six at the time, and had no idea that his mother and Frances had fallen in love years prior. Because of this man's presence in their lives before, it did not seem out of the ordinary to Paul that he followed the family to their new home.

As Paul grew up, he began to think of Frances as the person who taught their family about love. He lived an example of love; spoke the words of love. Frances left the priesthood for Lettie and his commitment to her seemed unwavering. Paul watched that example his whole life.

Paul heard speculation years later that his mother may have been taken advantage of by other priests in Kansas; it could have been one of the reasons the Dysarts left. Paul said that Frances knew about those indiscretions, and thought it could have influenced why he remained such a devoted man to Lettie Mae.

But he wasn't the only man. Scoop and Lettie moved to Sioux Falls as a family unit, and lived together with their children until Scoop's death in 1968. The secret that remained buried all those years was that Scoop and Lettie Dysart had gotten a divorce before moving to South Dakota. This fact was unknown to the children at the time; in fact, Paul didn't find out until he was 74 years old.

Looking back on childhood, Paul reflected on some of the family dynamics. His parents shared a room with twin beds. When Frances showed up, after spending a few weeks at the Star Hotel in downtown Sioux Falls, he soon moved in with the Dysarts and became a permanent fixture in the family circle. Paul said their family grew those years, adding four more children that lived under the Dysart roof.

The family never had more than a three bedroom home, the boys in one room, the girls in another.

With a smile Paul says, "When my brother and I were the same size, we'd share one pair of shoes—I'd have the left one day and he'd get the right."

He laughs at the absurdity, but his comment highlights his playful personality.

There is some discordance between the memories of childhood and the reality of it all. Paul knows with much certainty of his father's promiscuous behavior, citing a child born to his dad and Lettie's sister. Yet, his father tried to do right by his children.

Paul remembers hearing his mother and father come home late at night from the 20th Century Club, Paul describes it as the Black bar in Sioux Falls.

One night in particular, he recalls his parents arguing, voices raised as the door slammed shut behind them.

Scoop said to Lettie, "Look at us, both drinking and smoking with all these kids here — one of us has got to stop."

It turned out that Scoop would be the one to slow down on that lifestyle. Scoop had been a two or three pack a day smoker of Camel cigarettes. Paul remembers his mom liked Pall Malls, and later in the 1950's she switched to Viceroy cigarettes. Back in those days, ads ran headlines such as, "Reward yourself with the pleasure of smooth smoking" and "More doctors smoke Camels than any other cigarette."

Scoop and Lettie were part of a majority. Yet that night, drunk and reeking of cigarettes, Scoop knew it wasn't what was best for his family.

Paul listened from down the hall, snug in the bed he shared with his older brother. He pictured his mom and dad standing there, anger etched across their faces. There wasn't more than that though. His dad said he would stop and he did. Cold turkey. Scoop wouldn't smoke again. He didn't have a single drink until years later.

Life lesson: The examples we see growing up, shape and mold us.

Paul picked up on many subtle cues watching his father. Another moment that helped to shape Paul's view of the world was when the family wanted to purchase a home.

For the Dysart family every place they lived was a rental. It was in the 1950's that Scoop wanted to buy a home of his own. Paul was within ear shot when Scoop and a white lawyer exchanged heated words. The phrase that left a profound impact on young Paul, came from the white man.

He said, "As long as I see to it, your kind will never buy any property in this town."

Watching the words fly bitterly from the white man's face felt like a slap across the cheek to ten year old Paul, who silently observed. His father stood firm, although he didn't engage in back and forth insults. Even a child could see the moment would leave a lasting impression on Scoop, adding another layer to an already hardened heart. Scoop would never buy property in that town, or anywhere for that matter.

The Dysart family rented a place at First Street and Blauvelt. They didn't spend long in this dilapidated home in a run down part of Sioux Falls. The home was right next to the railroad tracks. The rumble of the train at night was easy to get use to, the low horn and the vibration that hummed through a person when one would be in bed. It was just background noise, like chirping birds and the whipping South Dakota wind.

From there, the family moved to 215 1/2 North Dakota Avenue. This was a home tucked in an alley behind Beck's Blacksmith Shop between Seventh and Eighth Street. After a while, the Dysarts moved again, renting a home in an alley off of Phillips Avenue down by the Falls of Sioux Falls. The row of houses could be described as "skid row" — Paul describes it as close to a ghetto as you could find in Sioux Falls at the time. When the family moved — Frances came, too. Paul remembers his mom told him not to tell anyone about Frances being a priest.

"That information ain't for anybody around here," she had said.

Paul was too busy being a kid, to think or care too much about who knew what of the adults in his life. Young Paul had a scooter, and he'd hide it in the weeds on top of Fifth Avenue. After school at St. Joseph's, he uncovered that small silver scooter and rode down Fifth Street with the wind in his hair and a smile on his face. The freedom of that speed made him oblivious to the danger, as cars would have to watch out for the young boy that could skate all the way down to Minnesota Avenue.

On occasion the Dysart children would walk to Mr. Page's place, just a half block away. The kids would take turns looking to see if the old man was around, and if he wasn't, the real fun began.

Paul, now about nine years old, would climb into the livestock pen in Mr. Page's city yard, gathering up the courage to wrangle a goat to ride. The wire fence scraped against his leg, and Paul turned to look at the small audience that gazed at him with admiration. He grinned and turned to face them on the inside of the fence now. Crouching down like the boxer he had seen on the tv down at the local bowling alley, he shouted, "Just call me Sugar Ray."

The kids laughed and waited for more. Once over the fence, Paul sauntered over to the goat in the corner, kicking up his heels for showmanship. He grabbed the goat by the horns and swung a leg over the skittish animal. The goat bleated and bucked, and the other children just rolled with laughter until rambunctious young Paul fell in the dirt.

Mr. Page, no doubt on more than one occasion, saw those little Dysart children and laughed at their antics. He kept the goats for milking, nearly a dozen right there in his front yard.

In about 1950 the Dysarts moved to 1127 North Dakota Avenue, next door ro the Kenny Anderson Family and three doors from the Anderson family of 11 kids. This home is where the "Legend of the Dysarts of the Dakotas" was born. The family spent 12 years in that home. Paul spent fifth grade through graduation there. The memories of family cards, Chitlin' feeds and being known as the welcoming place for all to gather is the home-life Paul chooses to remember most.

He recalls a lot of remodeling being done, but not when or how it was actually completed. At one point the family would have to walk through a bedroom to get to the bathroom, and then it changed. The kitchen was moved to the middle of the house, and the girls' bedroom to the back.

The kitchen was the center of family events, his mom would be cooking up something at the stove and the music would be playing. Lettie liked the female jazz singers, both she and Frances loved jazz music. The smooth sound of Dinah Washington's voice drifted from the kitchen many mornings.

The kitchen was colored a nicotine yellow, welcoming and familiar to Paul. Often his dad would mix-up his famous barbecue sauce. The sauce recipe was a family secret passed down from Paul's great-great grandad Finley after being freed as a slave.

Paul loved the story—after great-great grandad was freed, Finley grabbed the "sauce" recipe from the big house and began making it for his family and friends. The recipe has been passed from generation to generation ever since.

One thing Paul remembers, regardless of what was happening in life, food always seemed to bring folks together and their family sauce seem to make it, "just right."

The boys' room was a pale green color, two sets of bunk beds arranged on the east wall. Paul on one top bunk, Bobby on another. On the bottom beds were Frances on one side of the room and Larry on the other side.

Frances taught music for much of his life, teaching at St. Benedict's College in Kansas before coming to Sioux Falls. When Paul was young, Frances would entertain the kids by playing music with his hands, no instrument needed. Frances would cup his hands around his mouth and the sound of a trumpet or trombone was clear.

Paul watched Frances' commitment to the church his whole life. He estimates that Frances probably only missed attending church a dozen times in his entire life. Frances' father left their family when Frances was a young boy. His father was a traveling salesman and one day he just never came home, abandoning his wife and children. The Catholic Church helped him his whole life, and Frances felt obligated to pay them back, hence teaching at the college and continuing to send a check back to that church in Atchison, Kansas until the day he died.

Lettie was working as a domestic in the early 1950's for a wealthy family. There weren't many other options for employment for a woman of color. Lettie worked hard and she played hard. She would leave the house after her own children were off to school and then head to the Gridley's home where she cleaned their house, cooked their food and raised their children.

Lettie wasn't able to bring her own children when she went to work at the Gridley home. But in the summer she would have Paul come along to help with the dogs if the Gridley's were on vacation. The family had two big dogs, a Saint Bernard and a Great Dane.

Paul would go into the garage where the dogs, Felix and Dylan, enthusiastically greeted him. The big animals would lick his face as he tried to mix their food to the Gridley's specifications. He took a pound of raw hamburger, split that in two, adding it to the dry dog food and heaping in a scoop of cottage cheese. He mixed the dog's meal and set it down for the two monsters to munch.

Sometimes he and and his siblings would help his mom clean the windows at the big Gridley home, too. The home seemed to have 100 windows Paul said.

Lettie was not a loving mother, but her children knew she loved them. Perhaps, she used up all her patience on those other kids, or maybe she only knew one way to teach — however it was, Paul learned his lessons the hard way.

It was when Paul was 12 years old that he started as a newsie. Sioux Falls had a daily newspaper, the *Argus Leader*, dating back to about 1897. In the 1950's young boys were hired to buy the newspapers at about three cents apiece and then re-sell them for a nickel. The ink would rub off on

Paul's hands as he hauled the papers to his corner nearly each and every day.

He stood with the stack of newspapers at his feet at the corner of Eighth and Phillips. The Ronning Drug Store was on the corner and Hollywood Theatre down the street.

Paul would shout out, "*Argus Leader* paper... Five Cents..." in a tune that he made up.

He discovered a secret to sales: sell to the people most likely to buy.

Paul watched as day after day businessmen would get off work at 5 p.m. and head to a local bar. It didn't take long for Paul to notice that sales really picked up around 7 p.m. when those businessmen were happy.

"*Argus Leader*... Five Cents..." Paul sang out.

"Here ya go, kid," said a man in a black suit handing him a quarter, "Keep the paper."

With a pocketful of change Paul walked a block to the Sport Bowl. The bowling alley was two stories of fun for a young kid like Paul — arcade machines, bowling lanes and sweet treats. Paul discovered he had a liking for pinball. Not just a liking, an addiction.

"I'm next," Paul said laying a penny on the machine as he waited for a young boy to finish.

When it was his turn at the game, he dropped the copper in. His eyes lit up as he hit the paddles and guided the small silver ball around the machine, lights and sounds filling his head with happiness. The smell of freshly popped popcorn wafting over to him added to the enjoyment. Several kids would watch Paul as he would rack up the free games as his game play progressed. It wasn't until every cent was spent that he finally went home.

Even at the age of 12, Paul found out that gambling can be a problem. He spent weeks making money, and playing every cent he made on the pinball machines. Going home empty handed meant he would have to ask his mom for money to buy papers the next day.

Lettie would not stand for it.

She took Paul into his room and whooped him. The other kids gathered outside his door to hear him hollering.

"All I could think of was that pinball machine," Paul remembered.

It took about two weeks of that punishment before Paul finally curbed his appetite for playing at the arcade. When he came home the kids would run to the house and wait by the door — listening to find out if Paul had cut his own fate yet again.

Finally, he started coming home after the newspapers sold. Newsprint smeared on his hands, coins jingling in his pockets. Lesson learned for now.

The Dysart house had a coal furnace, there was a small window on the side of the house and a little chute to throw coal down. The furnace would fill the home with a warm, fiery smell. Paul accompanied his dad on several trips to get coal, even though it turned out to be a one way ride.

"Get in the car," Scoop said to his son.

Young Paul obliged, and hopped into the back seat of the light green 1953 Buick Roadmaster. He propped his arms on the back of the front seat and listened to his dad sing along to the car radio to the Matadors. Smokey Robinson was Scoop's favorite, he loved MoTown music.

When the Dysarts approached the coal yard, Scoop whispered to Paul, "Lay down in the back."

Paul laid down in the back seat hidden from view. Scoop drove over the scale to go get the load of coal. Once inside, Paul hopped out, helped his dad load up, and walked out of the rear entrance of the yard as his dad drove in the opposite direction toward the scale. Whatever Paul weighed, well that was the "extra coal" that Scoop didn't have to pay for.

Paul said they only pulled that ruse a few times.

Scoop didn't work long at the quarry, the job that brought his family to South Dakota. He worked for a time with Dan Coats, a prominent Black businessman in Sioux Falls, as prominent as a Black man was allowed to be at the time.

Later, thanks to his wife's connections over at the Gridley Home, Scoop was able to break into the cooking scene — hired by a neighbor of the Gridley's to work in the airport restaurant. It was at the old airport restaurant he was able to meet music legend Duke Ellington.

Later he was a cook at the Westward Ho Country Club. At one point Scoop tried to get a McDonald's franchise, but because of his skin color it was denied.

The first McDonald's in Sioux Falls was opened in 1961, at the southeast corner of 40th Street and Minnesota Avenue. It was the first McDonald's in the state, Max Pasley had purchased the local franchise.

It wasn't until 1968 that the color line was broken. It was that year that Herman Petty of Chicago, IL opened the first Black owned McDonald's franchise.

Paul was no stranger to work. Along with selling papers, he took his first real job at the age of 13. He was cleaning floors for Al Williams in downtown Sioux Falls at the Old Sportsman's Bar. The establishment was a big gambling place in the late 1950's and early 60's. Paul would scrub and clean the floors at night. The lessons he learned while working there, stayed with him for life.

His boss, Al came out one night behind the bar and honked.

Young Paul ran to the car, he said to the older man, "You gonna come in and check?"

Al looked at him and said, "What for? If I have to come and check it ain't worth having you."

The Life Lesson for Paul was the idea that a job is to be done right the first time.

He learned a lot about work in his early years. As a paper boy there was another time that he was educated in the art of debt collecting.

Paul was around 14 years old, still selling papers. There was a neighbor who asked Paul to leave a paper at his door each day, and Paul obliged. The man, Mr. Conrad, owed Paul $3. Paul saw him at Sport Bowl one day.

Mr. Conrad was a smallish man, though in his thirties he was shorter and leaner than teenage Paul. Paul and his friends were hanging out near the pinball machines when he saw him.

"Be right back," Paul said to the guys.

"Mr. Conrad," Paul said. The shorter white man began to look frightened as the young man approached.

"You owe me three bucks," stated Paul matter of factly.

Mr. Conrad's face flushed red and he slapped the boy across the face.

Paul's jaw clenched and his hands curled into fists at his side. Mr. Conrad took off running. Nothing came of it, Paul knew better than to give chase through the streets of downtown. He did try again to collect, this time stopping at the man's house.

Another life lesson: Don't ask for money in front of other people.

Paul learned much in his formative years on Dakota Avenue. In the basement of the house were several stacks of burlap sacks. Perfect hiding places, Paul thought. He hid a brown bag of money, hoping maybe to get it off his mind.

At St. Joseph's the day before, Paul had walked by the teacher's desk. On it sat a little brown bag filled with money. The empty classroom was too tempting — Paul grabbed the bag from the desk and pushed it down into his pocket. The lump of cash sat undisturbed until after the school bell rang.

He began to walk home, but stopped to contemplate. Paul sat under a large oak tree — hidden from view. He reached into his blue jean's pocket and counted the cash. Nearly $100 was folded in his hand. He was giddy with a mixture of excitement and nervousness. With the cash, Paul headed downtown.

He noticed a man walking.

He said, "Hey man, what would you do if you found some money?"

Paul dropped a $5 bill and walked away. He did that a few more times to watch the reaction of strangers with found money. Happiness at their surprised delight filled him each time the stranger reached down to pick up the cash.

The reality of having stolen money also began to seep into the cracks of that happiness, and it crumbled very quickly.

Paul headed home and ditched what remained of the stolen green in the basement. At school the next day, Paul's guilt got the better of him and when the nun asked the thief to come forward, Paul sheepishly stood and walked to the front of the classroom. He was escorted to the head office and his parents were notified.

That was the only time that his father whooped him. Scoop did not appreciate hearing from the school that his son was a thief.

Paul worked to pay back all of the money through selling newspapers, it took almost eight months. That was a life lesson for Paul learned the hard way: character matters.

There was time for work, and there was time for play.

The Falls of the Big Sioux River in Sioux Falls has been the center of recreation since the founding of the city in 1856. Now a developed city park, the Falls in the early years was unkept. There stood an old mill near the Falls, the Queen Bee Mill that was built in 1881. The seven-story structure was built of Sioux Quartzite that was quarried on site. Paul thought of his dad when he stared at the impressive building now used as a warehouse. His father worked at the quarry, and Paul had been there and watched the men work. To think something so strong and beautiful could be built from dynamite and dust. The mill closed in 1883, due to inadequate water power and a short supply of wheat. The mill was converted into a warehouse in 1929. Later, in 1956 a fire roared through the stone structure, destroying the wooden roof and interior floors. The upper walls were later knocked down to prevent them from falling.

Paul recalls summer afternoons at the Falls. Laying in the grass, feet dangling into the rushing water, and when the mood would strike, climbing around on the smooth pink quartzite rock. He and his friends would catch frogs in the tall green prairie grass. This delicacy was something they would cook up right there.

"I've got another one," Paul said as he handed a large frog to his friend.

The other boy laid the frog on a rock and cut the legs off with a pocket knife he pulled from his pocket, adding it to a skillet the boys had hidden in the grass, stashing it there for just such occasions.

Paul grabbed the Sterno canned heat that one of the boys had brought, the stick of butter that he had swiped from the Red Owl Grocery Store and he began to cook. The sizzle of the fresh frog legs crackled, and the delicious aroma drifted up from the little skillet as they waited. Paul had seen his mom and dad cook frog legs just like this many times. His dad was already teaching him how to make the family's famous meat sauce.

"The secret is safe with me," he told his dad.

His ma even told him that his sauce was turning out better than his dad's. He didn't know if she was just trying to make him feel good or if it was the truth, but he took the compliment and held on tight to it.

The boys laid outstretched on the grass after the feast of frog legs. The sun began to wear them down — and just like many other summer days, someone said, "Let's go swimming."

The group walked to the edge of the water and began taking off shirts. Paul was ready to cool off from the near 90 degree heat. It was a perfect July day, the sun was shining and the wind was light. Bill, Denny, and Paul split a $5.00 bill on two separate occasions diving off 30 feet at the Falls, earlier in the day. Then Paul looked to his left and noticed a clique of girls was at the Falls, too.

Paul shouted to his friends, "We got company."

He and the other boys looked at the five or six girls sitting near them.

"You gotta get outta here," Paul shouted to the girls, "We're going swimming."

"We don't have to leave," one girl said.

The boys looked at each other.

"You gotta go, we swim naked," Paul called out.

The girls giggled, shrugged their shoulders and pretended to ignore the boys.

Paul and the other boys figured they had tried to be gentlemen, and in a matter of minutes were stripped down and whooping and hollering in the water. A mere twenty minutes went by when Paul looked up and saw a police car approaching.

The boys scrambled out of the water to get their clothes on.

"What's going on here, fellas?" the officers asked.

"We were just swimming with our underwear on, sir," Paul lied.

"Now son," the officer said to Paul, singling out the only Black boy there, "I know you were not swimming in no white underwear."

All of the boys were taken down to the police station, although nothing came of it.

That summer, there was another run in with the local police. Paul and his friends were walking to Terrace Swimming Pool. Once again, Paul was the only Black kid in the group. Out of nowhere, a woman who was sitting on her porch began to shout insults at him.

"What you doing here, you Black son of a bitch," she shouted with a drink sloshing around in one hand.

The boys turned to look at this woman. Paul listened to a few more slanderous comments growing in anger and in tone, and then his patience broke.

"Shut up, you stupid whore," he began, as his friends just kept pulling him along, telling him to ignore the disrespect and verbal assault being hurled in his direction.

The boys were at the pool when the police showed up.

As the only Black kid in the pool, Paul wasn't hard to find. Officer Bob Gillespie came over to him.

"Son, you gotta come with me," he said, "We got a complaint you were harassing a woman."

Paul climbed out of the pool, said goodbye to his friends and rode in the police car to the station. Officer Gillespie was a nice man, but professional. They rode in silence.

Paul noticed the stares from people on the street as he looked out the backseat window. No doubt judgmental eyes only saw a teenage Black kid in trouble. Take him away, their faces seemed to shout.

At the station, Paul respectfully followed the officer into the sterile gray room.

As soon as they got to the front steps, Officer Gillespie said to Paul, "There's two things you do not do in this town and you'll be alright, you do not steal and you do not misuse their women."

Paul was free to go. As he walked home, Paul relived the day's events. The stupid woman, being wrongly accused, the stares from those white people.

He wondered, "Why can't we all just get along?"

Birthdays in the Dysart home were always celebrated — birthday cake, candles, and ice cream — for each of the nine kids. As they grew up, those parties evolved.

Teenage Paul, celebrating his 17th birthday was treated, not to cake and ice cream, but beer and booze. Paul said the only thing his mother asked, was that any of his friends who drank, stayed there.

His mom had made carrot cake, Paul's favorite. She kept his little siblings out of the way — although they were underfoot at every Dysart Party. Paul, himself, could remember falling asleep under a dining room table or two at his mother's feet. On this night, it was Paul at the kitchen table, he and his friends playing cards and drinking beer.

His friends, many of them classmates from St. Joseph's were often hanging out at the Dysart house, that is when they weren't shooting hoops. Paul was a decent basketball player.

During his senior year, St. Joseph's was in the state championship. The night of the tournament was one that Paul will never forget.

Paul grabbed his shoes, and was just heading out the door to get to the Colosseum in Sioux Falls, when the phone rang. Paul heard his mom answer the phone. Lettie said a few words and broke down in tears.

Paul paused at the door. He soon learned the heartbreaking news — his older sister, Doris and her one year old baby had been killed by a drunk driver. The accident occurred over by the golf course on East 10th Street. Five people died.

Paul sat at the kitchen table with his mother. Watching the tears roll down her face. The silence hung in the air; emotions heavy — Paul stood.

"My team needs me, Ma," he said walking out of the house.

The reality of not being able to do anything for his sister hung over him as he walked to the Colosseum. The cold February temperature in South Dakota went un-noticed.

He made his way to the locker room, as he entered Paul could see in his team-mates eyes the news had reached them before he did. No one talked of the tragedy. The coach just said, "Let's do this."

St. Joe came out on top that night, and the last person named to the All State squad was Paul Dysart. With the win, the team celebrated with a dance following the game. When Paul reached the top of the stairs looking down at the gym floor at good ol' St. Joseph High, other students applauded.

"It was as if I put the news of my sister's death in some portion of my brain and dealt with everything else at hand. You're aware of it, but it doesn't interfere with what you have to do," Paul said.

After Doris' death, Paul's father Scoop allowed himself one drink on the anniversary of her death every year until his own passing in 1968. Doris' little boy was named Matthew after her Grandpa. Doris was 18 years old.

Dances at St. Joseph's School were a challenge for Paul as the only Black student. The students voted Paul the Prince for the Press Ball, a tradition in which classmates nominated a Prince and Princess to be honored at the Dance.

r Oswin, the principal at the Catholic school called her office.

She sat across from him and said, "You know we don't allow our students to date girls from the other schools, but in your case we'll make an exception."

It was Paul's senior year, and up until that point, he had felt like just another Catholic kid at the school.

He replied, "Why sister? I think the girls here are just fine."

The sister's jaw dropped open.

She wrung her hands together and slowly said, "We'll allow you to get a date, perhaps a Black girl from Washington High School."

Paul, nonchalantly waved his hand, "Nah, I'll pass."

A white boy was chosen as the Prince for the dance, so as to stand next to the white Princess.

Paul dated a classmate at St. Joe's until her father put a stop to the interracial courting.

Paul would walk over to Joan's house to do home work and spend time together. They were classmates and neighbors. Her mother was always home and seemed friendly enough to Paul.

One night, Joan's father came home drunk and shouted at his daughter, "You can't have anything more to do with that boy."

The neighbors across the street had been giving him a hard time about allowing that Black boy to spend time with his white daughter.

Joan was crushed.

She called Paul that night and said, "I have to see you."

The two met at the top of Minnesota Avenue hill. She cried as she repeated the ugly words her father had said. Paul held her tight in a tender embrace. She was the one he had taken to the Press Ball, and he knew that was probably what got everyone talking. He wondered why people saw things so differently than he did.

Black athletes recall fighting for their rights

1960s Sioux Falls drew wide lines between races

SIOUX FALLS SD ARGUS LEADER 2006

Sports helped integration though, Paul said upon reflection.

As the article in the Sioux Falls, SD Argus leader of Sunday, Oct. 1, 2006 spells out about race relations in South Dakota sports, it brings Paul's thoughts back to how race was set aside on whatever field or court you were on, dating back to his 6th, 7th, and 8th grade basketball participation in the local YMCA program. Those years were highlighted with being the only Black athlete, and his dear buddy Willie Brave, the only Native American on their two different yearly championships. Race wasn't an issue.

Moving on to high school, Paul's biggest memory that hasn't faded a bit, is about finally going out his senior year for basketball and making the starting five. He recalls clearly being around the open door of coach Leo Dolan's office to hear a very irate Catholic parent yelling at coach saying, "You mean to tell me you are going to start that f***ing n****r instead of my red haired Catholic boy!"

Paul never shared what he heard with anyone, but found out years later another student heard it and quietly spread the word unbeknownst to Paul. Race began to become an issue.

The life lesson for Paul was that though things may appear to be okay on the surface, often deeper issues may be afoot.

The next step in sports led to Paul playing on the South Korean Army championship team of Korean Military

Advisory Group, Wonju Korea and winning the league MVP in 1960. Move on to FT Devens, MA fondly playing on the 1st Army Championship team in 1961. In the US military, race wasn't an issue.

Paul was honorably discharged in 1962 and began playing fast pitch softball winning the state championship with Lyles Champlian, 1965 and SF Merchants, 1970. Paul played all positions, but primarily first base or catcher, grabbing a couple all-state honors through the fastpitch years of 1962 to 1980. Race wasn't an issue.

From 1950 to 1980, the escape into the world of sports learning how to compete, win, lose, and appreciate the efforts of all participants helped place Paul in a world alongside the real world, as it is presented to people of color where race is an issue.

Old age and limited mobility allows Paul to pursue his last sport participation which is Cribbage. As a member of the American Cribbage Congress for the past 15 years and two club champion years, he sends a shout of thanks out to Terry, Dan, Don, Roger, Buck, Cindy, Loellen, Wayne, Aaron, and all three Petersons. Once again, race wasn't an issue.

Life Lessons (1958)

Paul says often he didn't, and doesn't, think of the color of his skin. But he's no stranger to prejudice and has had plenty of experiences that highlight the ugliness of racism. After high school Paul joined the Army, serving three years, three months and four days from Sept. 1958 to Jan. 1962.

Before he left for service in Korea he recalls a moment in downtown Sioux Falls on Eight and Main Street, at the Boston Cafe. The restaurant was beside the Look's Meat Market. Paul walked in, intending to order a burger.

"I wasn't a Catholic kid anymore, I became the N-word," he said.

Paul stepped up to order.

The white man, with a white apron stood behind the counter, judgment in his stance, and said, "We don't serve your kind here."

Paul, a strapping 18 year old, defiantly answered back, "You don't serve me, you ain't gonna serve nobody."

Another employee in the Meat Market called the Sioux Falls Police Department, no doubt in an effort to avoid confrontation. It was local officer Gillespie and according to Paul he showed up on the right law.

Gillespie said, "This boy's right, you have to close this place up if you don't serve him."

Paul got his burger.

This wasn't the only incidence of discrimination Paul faced in Sioux Falls. He recalled another time at Ray's Place. The establishment was out on West Twelfth Street, across the street from Kirk's Restaurant where a Dairy Queen sits now. The same thing happened, the man behind the counter refused to take his order. The law was called, again it was Gillespie who showed up again.

Paul said that while in Sioux Falls he often gravitated toward other African Americans, the one thing that set his family apart though was his Catholic upbringing.

He said, "We were brothers and sisters because there wasn't very many of us. You acknowledge one another because you're in a a pool of liquid and you're a different type, you don't just blend in. When you encounter another, it's like we know the burden of this pool we're in."

Because of his Catholicism, the blending in to the Black community was just a bit harder. Although he credits being raised Catholic as giving him the ability to lighten up nearly every situation.

One instance he recalls in Sioux Falls was at a local bar with a fellow Black man, Mike Harris. He and Paul were waiting with fellow teammates, all white, to go play a softball tourney. A young boy came in ready to shine shoes.

Paul smiled at the young boy, probably just ten years old.

Mike stuck his shoe out for the lad to shine.

The little boy looked up at the man and grabbed his cloth with a smile.

He said, "I'll make it shine like the N-word's heel."

Mike's face froze, and Paul quickly chimed in, "You mean like a Norwegian heel, don't ya?"

The boy smiled, "Yes, sir."

And all the white customers and players laughed and moved on.

Tensions were high, but Paul found that a light touch often offered better results. Life Lesson: Humor is a tool used to defuse many situations.

Paul left for the Army in September of 1958. He went to Fort Carson, Colorado. He didn't know anyone at the time. He trained in Colorado for two months and from Fort Carson, headed to Fort Leonard Wood, Missouri. Paul came home in December for the holidays. During this break, Paul got together with some friends, two of whom wanted to get married — Jake and Cathy. Jake asked Paul to drive the couple up to Pipestone to get hitched on New Year's Eve,

Paul brought along his girl, a white girl he had been spending time with before leaving for the military, Darlene.

The four foolhardy young adults got to the Justice of the Peace as the snow was falling. Jake and Cathy said I do, and on whim, Jake said to Paul, "You two ought to get married, too."

Paul said, "Why not!"

He and Darlene had not even kissed, yet incredibly, Darlene went along with the marriage proposal. The four happy teenagers headed back to Sioux Falls, Paul dropped her off at home and headed back to his parent's place, wondering what just happened.

The next day, Paul and his father were out for a drive.

Paul said to Scoop, "What would you say if I married a white woman?"

Scoop didn't take his hands off the wheel, and said, "I'd ring your fucking neck."

Paul sunk back into his seat and didn't say another word.

Paul went back to the service to continue training. He went to Fort Ord, California. Although Paul and Darlene never consummated their marriage, by law she was his wife. Because of this, his checks from the service were going to her back in Sioux Falls. Paul was going to be deployed to Korea, and he knew — he needed to get his marriage annulled.

Paul called Darleen, who agreed, and they quickly annulled their hasty marriage.

Soon after, during mail call, Paul was happy to get a letter from his dad.

He sat down on his cot later that day to read it, as he unfolded the letter a newspaper clipping fell into his lap: *Annulment Records*. The only words hand-written by Scoop were, "At least you could have told old Dad."

On another visit home while serving, Paul did talk to his dad about it.

"You remember," Paul began, "When we were riding around and I asked you about marrying a white woman? You remember what you said?"

Scoop sighed.

He said, "You know what I meant was if you got a difference of religion there's a problem, but a Black person and white person is just adding extra burden to the marriage and marriage is tough enough."

Back in the service again, Paul was recruited for the army's basketball team. His basketball talent was well known. One game he remembers vividly was in Fort Devens, Massachusetts, a United States Army Reserve military installation in the towns of Ayer and Shirley. At this game he got into a fight with none other than Lenny Wilkens. Leonard Randolph "Lenny" Wilkens is an American retired basketball player and coach in the National Basketball Association.

As his opponent, and a shorter scorer than he, Paul said a few words to get his motor going, ultimately causing a fight and getting both of their points thrown out. Paul laughed as he recalled his eight points didn't compare to Lenny's 33.

That same year Paul's team won the first Army Championship in 1961. The commander was so appreciative that the entire team was awarded a tour through the southern states. The tour was something that educated the young 20 year old from South Dakota. Paul said it was the first time in his life that he read a sign that said, "No N-word or dogs allowed." The sign was on the front door of a restaurant in North Carolina.

Another moment etched into memory was at a cafe. Paul was one of four Black men on the basketball team, and Barry, as Paul described, was half-Black.

Paul laughed, "Barry was always sleeping every time we got south of D.C. to stop and eat. He didn't want to face the degradation of being challenged. He was getting by as white. He was very sensitive about rocking the boat."

Paul was the only Black man from South Dakota on the team, all the other men were from the south. The day they stopped at this cafe, Paul was the first to go in and he thought nothing of it.

He said when he entered the cafe, he looked around at the white faces of the diners and heard silverware hit the floor.

"It was like I spoiled their meals," he recalls.

The group of 12 or 15 Army men took seats at the counter, the other Black men in the company all headed to the bathroom, leaving Paul to sit at the counter. Paul noticed five Black faces looking out of the kitchen directly at him. Food orders started coming to the other men.

Paul's captain walked over to him and asked, "Aren't you eating?"

Paul replied, "Sir, she won't take my order."

The captain walked to the waitress and said, "We are the United States Army, you either serve him or you just gave out a lot of food for free."

Paul ordered to the disdain of the waitress. The other Black men who had been hiding out in the bathroom walked out with their heads held high and also placed their orders, locking eyes with Paul and taking their seats at the counter.

That day Paul learned about the power of advocates.

Paul said little about his time in Korea serving with his unit.

He said, "In 1960 Korea there was a lot that $2.20 could buy you. How do you keep young men full of piss and vinegar in line? Give them their liquor and their women, and all is well."

Paul received his honorable discharge from the U.S. Army and returned home to Sioux Falls in 1962.

Paul stayed at his parents place, and Frances, as always, was there. Homelife was as he remembered, but the home was larger. Now the Dysarts resided in a six bedroom home, near Fifth and Spring, just below the Cathedral.

One of the neighbors happened to be the family of Buddy Miles. The Miles family was another African American family from Kansas. Buddy, back then 15 years old, would go on to become a famous American rock drummer, vocalist, composer and producer, playing with Jimi Hendrix, Carlos Santana and others.

Paul's younger sister, Carlotta, told Paul the story of how they would dance like the Supremes to his music.

Lettie and Buddy's father George had a falling out, unbeknownst to Paul at the time. George had apparently gotten frisky with one of Lettie's girls. This didn't sit well with Ma.

By the time Paul came home he entered in to an unknown landscape of relationships and back stories that he had missed. It left the 22 year old in a hard position. One moment changed things permanently.

George's wife stopped by the Dysart home, and said, "Lettie, you got something to drink?"

Paul was a silent observer in the large living room with the big round window looking out at the street.

"Yea," Lettie answered, "you go in the kitchen there get a beer and get the hell out."

The woman did just that, and Paul wondered why she didn't just keep walking, but trouble often stirs until it bubbles to the top. The two women stood face to face. Paul had no idea what had transpired before this moment, but knew that what would come next would not be good.

Lettie began wailing on the woman. Paul stood, frozen in place, watching these two 40 year old women brawl.

Finally, Paul spoke, "Mom, that's enough."

At six foot one and Army fit, it was nothing for Paul to pull his mother off the other woman, left cowering in the corner of the living room.

In the heat of the moment, Lettie smacked Paul right across the face, and in an instant reaction Paul smacked her back.

The reaction and the situation was explosive, more charged than the ammunition that Paul learned to handle in the service. That moment only solidified his place, which was no longer there. Leaving home that time was harder somehow, permanent and sorrowful.

Fifty-four years later, Paul lowers his voice and says, "It was the worst thing I ever did in my life."

The life lesson for him was that an ill-advised moment carries lasting impressions.

Paul moved out; his dad moved out with him for a time, and they stayed at the Williams' house. Scoop ended up back at the family's home, and Paul got an apartment.

He didn't let himself off easy, reliving that moment and asking the question, "What the hell did you do?"

Wishing he had wrapped his mother up and held her, instead of reacting the way he did. But the reflex was immediate, and as it turned out, not permanent. Their relationship was repaired.

Years later, when Lettie was sick and in the hospital, which was a rare occurrence, Paul never even knew her to go to a hospital before, he brought up the painful incident.

Paul walked in to her hospital room with a dozen red roses in hand.

He looked at his mother, a great deal older now. She seemed much smaller and more fragile than he remembered her to be.

"Mom, I never told ya how sorry I was when I reacted to your fight with Mrs. Miles," he said softly.

Lettie touched her boy's hand, "Son, you don't have to say nothing."

Paul's tears flowed, it was as if there had been some infection in him and the tears washed it out. She recovered and they became closer. Being a good looking one-quarter Native American and three-quarter Black woman with nine Black children in the 1940's and 50's in South Dakota, Lettie struggled with gambling and alcohol most of her life. She died in 1994.

Settling Down (1962)

At the age of 22, Paul was ready to settle down, and this time he looked to the eligible African American women in Sioux Falls, thinking back to his father's advice.

Paul asked Brenda Hayes to marry him, she was the preacher's daughter. Mr. Hayes was a pastor at St. John's Baptist Church. She agreed. Three beautiful children were born to the union that lasted eight years.

Paul and Brenda married in 1962. Now married and looking for a way to support his family, Paul turned his energy to finding a job. For a brief time he and Brenda lived with her parents, Paul was working at Mundt's Cabinet Shop making $1.25 an hour. The cabinet shop was located on North Chicago Avenue between Fifth and Sixth Streets. Paul would go to houses, measure walls, go back to the shop, draw out what the homeowner wanted, build the cabinets and install them — all for $1.25 an hour. He knew he needed more.

He had a lot of friends who worked at John Morrell's Meat Packing Plant in Sioux Falls, where the starting pay was $4.00 an hour. Paul's eventual step-father Frances worked at John Morrell's for over 30 years. Frances and Lettie were married in 1969, after Paul's father, Scoop passed away in 1968.

Morrell's didn't hire Blacks in the 1960's. Yet, Paul persisted. He went to Morrell's three times a week to update his application, seeing other white men get hired all the time. Finally, with the help of Frances and other union men, Francis McDonald and Frank Olson, the company hired Paul as their first Black employee in 1964.

Although happy he got the job, it was short lived. Going home after his first day, Brenda told him the Post Office called and wanted him now. He went that afternoon to talk with Post Master Howard Wood. The Civil Rights Act of 1964 had just created the U.S. Equal Employment Opportunity Commission (EEOC); because of this, the Post Office was looking to hire minorities. Paul couldn't refuse the offer, and gave his two weeks notice to Morrell's.

Paul said the decision to leave wasn't hard. His job at Morrell's was washing beef, stripping hide and hanging it on a big chain. He was soaked in that, he recalled. To move to a position with the United States Post Office, a government job with benefits, was just a wise decision.

No one said much to Paul about leaving. It could have had something to do with his intimidating stance, at six foot one and 230 pounds of muscle.

Paul started work at the United State Postal Service in 1964. He started on the dock, unloading trucks.

Paul doesn't pretend he was an ideal husband or father during this time in his life, he'd had an affair that led to another child.

He and Brenda were ready to part ways in about 1970.

The other woman, Shirley, with whom he had the affair was married. She told Paul she intended to leave her husband to be with him when she found out she was pregnant with their child. There was no doubt it was his child. Paul and Shirley had only violated their vows on a few occasions.

She broke the news about the affair to her husband, and the news about the pregnancy, explaining who Paul was. The moment went as a person would expect — terrible.

Shirley's husband reacted in anger and grabbed a gun. He headed straight to where he knew Paul would be. He lurked around the block of Paul's house where Shirley eventually found him and coaxed him into going home. Paul didn't even know the imminent threat that awaited him outside.

That incident led Shirley back to her husband's side. He later tried to over-dose and she ended up staying with him permanently. Shirley left town to have Paul's baby, telling her family that her baby died in childbirth, and she adopted a Puerto Rican family's baby that was up for adoption in an effort to explain the baby's darker skin tone.

Paul would see his daughter around town, but never once said anything. He felt it was Shirley's decision.

Because Shirley's husband turned out to be a class act, Paul realized his sperm donating indiscretion put him in the very proud-father-from-a-distance position

It was not until their child was 18 years old that the truth was revealed.

Nicole, Paul and Shirley's daughter, was told the truth as a senior in high school after she had started asking questions. She was only a year apart from Paul's son, Paul Jr. and they knew each other well. Once she found out the truth, she met up with Paul Jr. at the Macomba Club.

She said, "Can you keep a secret?"

With Paul Jr.'s nod, she whispered in his ear, "I'm your half sister."

The news didn't take long to travel back to Paul Sr. He recalls that he received a phone call from Paul Jr. who had called his sisters and they'd met up at the Oasis Tavern, an all night bar in Sioux Falls, where one could bring their own bottle in and drink the night away. The kids, all young adults now, demanded to know the whole story.

Paul went right over that night to set the record straight. These days, his relationship with his daughter is good, and she maintains her close relationship with her mother and adoptive father as well.

During this time in his work life, there was an opportunity for Paul to move up to management in the Post Office. To Paul that meant sacrificing the way he did things, and the relationships he had with his co-workers. He didn't want to be a snitch just to move up the ladder he said. So without a plan, he quit the United States Postal Service.

Timing is everything, and it was about two weeks after Paul left the post office that there was a knock on his door.

A large white man from IBM in Sioux Falls was at the door. The first thing he said to Paul was, "We're not looking to put a N-word in the window."

Paul said he thought about punching the man right then, but he didn't, and heard the man's piece. As it turned out they needed to replace a Black employee that left because his wife didn't want to raise their child in South Dakota. So Paul began at IBM in 1970.

The office was over on West Avenue and his job title was customer engineer. He fixed office machines.

"Basically, I was a repair man," he said.

"I'd go to offices and the women would tell me the dictaphone was broke, or the typewriter. And here I am in my tie and suit," he said with a smile, "There was advantages to that, things we don't talk about."

He said that he felt his ability to "not sound Black" was what attributed to his success there and the company wanted him to follow the management track. Yet once again, Paul wasn't ready to follow the path others picked out for him.

"I was ready for sales, I knew more money was to be made," he said.

Management though, disagreed.

His boss said, "Black people can't sell in this part of the country."

Paul's response was, "You and I can go to a prospective client in this part of the country, right off the bat and I have his attention. All I have to do is start talking, whachatalkinabout?"

Paul left IBM in 1976.

After IBM, Paul needed something different. His kids and ex-wife were in Denver, so he had freedom and a longing to do more, but he wasn't quite sure what that was yet.

He worked as a bouncer at Seven Oaks for a time. He got that job after meeting one of the waitresses there — Leslie. His time with her is remembered fondly, it was for nearly eight years off and on they would be together. Paul defines her as the one who taught him about love.

Saying I love you became easier. One moment that replays in his mind was in the early 70's. Paul recalls talking to his mom, ready to leave after a Sunday visit.

He turned and said to her, "Good bye, Mom, I love you."

It was a minute the two stared at each other. Love wasn't a word that was heard often in his family. But this was a break through.

Lettie looked at her grown son and answered back, "I love you too, Paul."

A life lesson in the power of words — I love you. Those three words, spoken with sincerity can demonstrate support, encouragement, and acceptance.

Making Changes (1976)

From paper boy to meat washer, from the post office to IBM — Paul was ready for something new in his career. It was about 1976 that he and his cousin, Porter Williams started the company PP Inc. Paul describes the venture as becoming a "Black Gypsy."

Porter converted an old school bus into a colorful caravan and he and Paul drove down to Tijuana, Mexico to purchase pottery, paintings, onyx figures, leather goods, etc. The two would come back to Sioux Falls and sell their wares at P&P Imports, a little store on Twelfth Street. They made the trip several times a year.

Porter had a brother in San Diego, so they stopped there, the young men took turns driving, while the other slept.

Paul says, "We were the Black Cheech and Chong."

One trip was especially memorable. Paul was driving on the outskirts of Bakersville, California, when suddenly the bus shuddered and smoke billowed from the engine. Paul knew the engine had blown. Nothing could be done but to pull over.

The trucker that had trailed behind them offered to pull the bus up the hill. They coasted into Bakersville. Paul and Porter called around to junkyards and found a motor they thought could work. An old mechanic helped them out — but the two were stranded there for nearly a week. The hippie bus and the two Black Gypsies, camped out right near the mechanics shop.

For about nine months, Paul made the trips with Porter, filling the bus with leather goods and bringing it all back to their Twelfth Street store, selling items for as much as 600% mark-up.

Paul recalls a time when he sold the popular black velvet paintings from a street corner in Minneapolis. A callback to his newsboy days.

Selling was a way to make a living. In 1976 the South Dakota centennial was happening. Paul came across one of those black velvet paintings with Mount Rushmore painted on it, not just one painting but 150. Thinking he could make a killing, he bought all they had. Paul hoped to get one of the stores out west to purchase them from him, instead he discovered a lesson in marketing. All of those places had their orders for centennial products long ago. He ended up hawking the paintings himself like he always did.

After a few months their little market dried up as bigger department stores started carrying the same types of items. The opportunity had disappeared.

Around this time, Leslie introduced Paul to her uncle. He owned land in Sioux Falls that was prime development space.

Paul had big ideas. After he had gotten out of the Army he had joined the Seabees. One of the recruiters was Don Dunham, a well-known name in real estate on the local scene.

There was an understanding if Paul were to get his real estate license he would be able to get in on a deal with Leslie's uncle's property. The development potential was substantial. Paul was proposed a small percentage of every lot, and the numbers made sense. He went to Pierre to get his Realtor's license. Paul returned to Sioux Falls as the first Black Realtor in the State of South Dakota, Feb. 6, 1978.

The development plan fell through upon his return with license in hand. Paul was cut out of the deal on that parcel of land that parlayed all of the players into the biggest names in real estate in Sioux Falls and South Dakota.

Paul left Sioux Falls to head down to Kansas City to visit his sister. She was having a hard time with a boyfriend and Paul knew he needed to check things out. Paul was recovering from back surgery after having a disk removed, and thought the change of scenery would do him good. In the winter of 1976 Paul had slipped and re-injured his back. It aggravated the chronic back pain that was an issue he had dealt with since his army days following a fall out of a truck.

While in Kansas City, Paul was arrested with 32 white crosses in his pocket, the street name for the prescription drug Dexedrine, a form of amphetamine or speed. Named after the cross shape pressed into the top of the pill so it can be divided into quarters.

He didn't have a prescription. He only had the angry ex-boyfriend of his sister and enough illegal drugs in his pocket to get him five years in prison. With no priors and a good lawyer, Paul was able to walk away with a five year suspended sentence.

He left Kansas City and didn't look back. He continued to pursue his real estate career trying to shake the chip that rested on his shoulder. He interviewed at another real estate office.

The man performing the interview sat behind a large oak desk. He looked over Paul's resume and looked over him.

He said, "You have no experience in sales. What makes you think you can sell."

With confidence Paul said, "I can sell because you can sell. I can do anything you can do."

The man, a white man in a suit, was impressed with the self-assured attitude.

"End of conversation," he said, "When can you start?"

Paul smiled back, "I could use a car."

His new boss leased Paul a Lincoln that very first week and Paul sold a house for $65,000. It was a great first year. He felt secure and enjoyed the success.

However, there was always something lurking; a reminder of judgement. Sometimes a little jab, other times a punch in the face.

He spent some time bartending at the Edsalear bar on 12th Street downtown Sioux Falls, SD, as one of the very first Black people to bartend in Sioux Falls outside of the infamous 20th Century Bar, which was located on Phillips Ave between Fifth and Sixth Street. The 20th Century Bar was where the ladies were upstairs and the gamblers were downstairs. The bar on the main floor was the "forbidden fruit" kind of establishment that was popular during the '30s through the '60s in Sioux Falls. Early on, Paul recognized that the way to create the right atmosphere in bar settings was to mix the music with the people to go with the drinking. It didn't take long for Paul to begin creating some good vibes during his shifts and the bar became a place to go.

One of the customers, Kenny, began coming pretty regularly and sat at the same stool for about two or three weeks. Paul recalled that Kenny liked the same drink as his mom.

When she came in, she would loudly proclaim, "I just got here. I'll have a black jack with a water back."

Which was Paul's clue to play BB King — "Bring it on home." No matter what time she came in the mood in the bar became incredibly jovial. Once Paul's mom found out that Kenny and her shared the liking for the same drink, whenever they were both in, it was a drink exchange, which led to some conversations about several different topics.

With Kenny's southern accent he brought from Tennessee and the fact, that as a bartender, Paul was able to help break the ice for him with a few of the young ladies that came in. Paul didn't realize how Kenny felt about race, as he and 98% of the clientele were white.

Paul remembered, "Until I looked into the mirror it didn't always dawn on me that I am Black."

One night Kenny came in, took his stool and Paul poured him a black jack with water back. He had a brown paper bag that he set down by his feet as he drank about three. He called Paul over and said he wanted to give him something but he didn't want any of the others to see.

"We went to the office where he opened the bag and said he never thought he would have gotten himself to this place in his mind if he had not witnessed all that he had witnessed coming to this bar," Paul recalls the moment. "He went on to say how sorry he was for the way he had been living his life, traveling and working throughout the south. He wanted to let me know he was moving on to another location, but felt he had to give me the contents of the bag because he said he truly believed if he left it here, as he said, he could indeed leave it here. He admitted to participating in some unmentioned acts and somehow felt this was the right time and right place for him to free himself. He wanted me to be the one to accept and destroy the contents of the brown bag."

Paul stood in silence as all he could see inside the bag was white material. Kenny pulled out a full KKK outfit.

Then he stuffed it back into the bag and looked at Paul and said, "Thanks man."

The two men gave each other a hug. It was the last time they saw each other. The outfit (pictured below) has remained in the bag for over 40 years waiting for the right time and place for Paul to burn it.

That experience taught Paul that people can change when they are exposed to their ignorance.

The Klan wasn't unique to the south, according to the Sioux Falls Daily Press dated July 1, 1921, the Klan began to appear in the Sioux Falls area when an out of state promoter actively recruited new members. From its beginning, when the Ku Klux Klan arose from the ashes of the Civil War, until the present, the Klan has had a history of 140-years of bigotry, hatred, violence, intolerance, and ignorance

The dark cloud of racism didn't seem to lift, even when years went by, and the city seemed to become more progressive.

A stark reminder of the trials he faced as a Black man came from two old spinster ladies who had called the real estate office looking for a Realtor to help sell their home. It was 1980 in Sioux Falls, Paul went to their large two story home in the McKennan Park area of Sioux Falls. As soon as he came to the door to greet them, the grey haired woman looked him up and down.

Her lips were drawn in a straight line and she didn't blink an eye as she said, "I don't want no N-word in my house."

Paul didn't stumble over his words; he snapped back and turned on his heels to leave. He knew it wasn't worth wasting his time.

Time was valuable. He had met another girl — Katie. She was interesting, she was beautiful and she and Paul loved to spend time together. Paul even talked her into going into real estate. Before long, she and Paul moved in together.

One summer day as Paul was working at Edsaler's Bar he looked out the window and there stood his oldest daughter and oldest son, each with a suitcase in hand. He greeted his ex-wife in the parking lot.

"I've taken it this far," she told him.

His two kids moved in with his girlfriend and her two children, expanding the blended family as best they could. The situation wasn't ideal though, and Paul felt it was best for he and his children to find their own home. Paul found a place to rent on the east side of Sioux Falls at Ninth and Wayland.

Another well known bar owner, Bill Struck, became friends with Paul and Paul would often run errands for him. He spent entire days driving Bill where he needed to go — once Paul drove him all the way to Arizona to check on his condo. Life was interesting.

With his real estate career still going and his part-time gigs at the bars filling in the gaps, Paul was living the high life.

At this time though, Paul was aware of the bigger picture. During the 1960s, America was going through some real changes — influenced, mainly by the Vietnam War.

Paul was discharged from the US Army in February 1962. After he watched the abuse of his fellow veterans during the Vietnam War he decided to join the US Navy Seabee reserve in 1964 to 1970.

Paul lost one of his best buddies in the war in 1966, his friend was white. Paul wasn't able to be a best man at his wedding years earlier, and he couldn't be a pallbearer in his funeral, due to the color of his own skin.

"My first experience with marijuana was with some of the returning veterans in 1964. During the 60's and 70's us baby boomers were experimenting with all kinds of drugs. We knew who to go to get what party drug we wanted. Unknown to me, my landlord was busted by the Drug Enforcement Administration (DEA) for selling some pot. To get out of his mess, he had to call any user he knew to get other drugs. When he called me I told him I would check around for him. I found someone who could get him some coke. He told me a friend would come and get it. I got some a couple times and for him. During a 30 day stretch. he called me over 25 times to find him whatever drugs I could. At the end of about 30 days I agreed to get him some coke one more time. I was set up to meet him at Renchler's truck stop. When I showed up I was arrested for sales of coke. I was taken to the police station and I was offered the same deal my landlord got — to give the names of all my contacts, or anybody I knew that could score." Paul remembers.

He recalls sitting in the basement of the jail and listening to their offer.

"You have an opportunity here," they began, "just give up ten people and we'll make it easy on you."

Paul knew he couldn't give up his friends.

His philosophy, "You do the crime, you do the time."

But he did agree to go with the agents to point out a couple of the key players at a local Club.

When he would approach the men at the club, Paul would only whisper, "Shit's getting hot, lay low, get rid of what you got."

The police let Paul stay out of jail to make these contacts. Biweekly he had to meet the officers at a motel and give them names. After it became evident that he wasn't cooperating, they made a public announcement on St. Patrick's Day 1981. The 6 o'clock news ran the story — Dysart arrested for selling cocaine.

The outlook was grim, with Paul's prior arrest just five years earlier he knew it wouldn't be a slap on the wrist this time.

The Prison Experience (1982)

In September 1982 Paul appeared before Judge Gene Paul Keane. The State's Attorney told the judge that Paul should get 10 years in prison because he didn't respect the drug laws.

Of course, Paul knew many other's that didn't respect those laws either. There was a period of time that some well known people were really worried.

"I'm talking lawyers, policemen, and prominent business people," said Paul. "A friend had a picture of the South Dakota State's Attorney smoking a joint, and it was known that his appetite for coke was ten times larger than mine."

Paul was sentenced to three years in the SD State Penitentiary. After doing 11 months, he was taken to Pierre to appear before the grand jury, where he was asked one question, "Mr. Dysart if you wanted to buy some coke who would you contact?"

Paul looked the Attorney General right in the eye and gave him the name of the Minnehaha States Attorney.

Of course this resulted in, "no further questions" and Paul was brought back to the Pen. Authorities called the

Missouri State Penitentiary and told them to impose that five year sentence Paul had received five years prior in Kansas City, MO for possession.

So as Paul was preparing for discharge from the South Dakota Penitentiary, two officers just loaded him up and took him to Jefferson City, MO to the Missouri State Pen, where he would serve another year and a half. Paul was released on Jan. 15, 1985.

South Dakota prison life wasn't overly hard for Paul. Standing six feet tall and built solid at 250 pounds, he was able to handle himself and appear intimidating even if he had no intention of causing issue.

He recalls that the jail cell clinging wasn't that dramatic, but when the door slammed it was like a mirror right in front of you, a reflection that would cause a person to question just how one ends up in a place like that.

Paul had only two physical encounters in South Dakota.

"The guards made me a runner, which is like a trustee who is out of his cell, who sweeps the walkway and takes things to the inmates that are locked down," Paul explained. "On one floor there was a mix of bikers and white supremacists who really hate people of color."

After a week of sweeping up trash on their floor Paul had enough of the comments, and knew something had to be done. Paul had the support of Captain Frank. The Captain had told Paul, "Do what you need to do."

Paul said, "I was able to be placed in an area with the leader of the group. It took less than half a minute to really kick his ass, and there were no problems from that point on."

But if Paul learned anything from prison, it was that South Dakota wasn't as challenging as Jefferson City, Missouri.

"It's a fact that doing time in South Dakota was really closer to a strict Boy Scout camp," said Paul

In Missouri, Paul vividly recalls sitting at lunch while at a table away a man was stabbed.

Another incident that shaped his experience was a near miss. Paul started attending Catholic service on Sundays in prison. Unbeknownst to him, this Mass service was being used as a gathering of a wing of the Aryan Brotherhood. Which is a white prison gang and organized crime syndicate in the United States. Of course, Paul, as a Black man was not welcome.

He recalls one Sunday the prisoners were not let out of their cells to attend Mass, the same thing happened the following week. On the third week, when they were finally allowed back to the Mass, Paul asked the Priest why they were not allowed for two weeks?

He lead Paul to a quiet corner of the room.

"There was an attempt on your life," the Priest explained.

A knife had been stashed in the room where Mass was held and a plan constructed that included someone from the Brotherhood jump Paul and stab him to death. The Priest reluctantly confided to Paul that one of the Aryan Brotherhood members felt guilty over the idea and had warned the Priest.

That small act by that one white man, undoubtedly saved Paul's life.

"The longer I thought about it, the luckier I felt."

Paul knew that should something like that have happened it no doubt would have been written up as another "race incident." After an internal investigation, several of the Brotherhood members were transferred to other institutions.

Another incident occurred as Paul was clerking for the Captain of the "hole." The "hole" refers to solitary confinement. It's well-known that prisoners are routinely tossed in the hole based on attitude or color.

One day, Paul spotted a large shank stashed in the Captain's office. He knew it was out of place, and felt he had better alert the Captain to it. So he discreetly pointed it out to the Captain.

After investigation, the Captain was able to trace the weapon back to several prisoners, a few of the "hole" regulars. Once they were found out, they were transferred. The moment helped to highlight Paul's strength of character to those in charge, as well.

Life is at a different level in prison Paul learned.

"You learn how to get along, you learn how to tolerate the food, do your time one day at a time, you learn to get along with all kinds of stuff," Paul said.

In Missouri, Paul worked his way up to be a trustee at the Governor's Mansion, working for then Governor, Kit Bond.

The benefit for Paul was getting to leave the prison. Paul was on the detail to help cook and clean at the Mansion. Miss May ran the Governor's Mansion, Paul said he would help put out a six or seven course meal, along with five other inmates that went to the Mansion daily.

One of his favorite dishes he learned to make while there was the Current River Sheetcake from the cookbook "Past & Repast the history and hospitality of the Missouri Governor's Mansion," Copyright 1983. Once the party was over at the Mansion, Paul would sneak a few pieces back to the boys at the prison.

Paul learned a lot under the tutelage of Miss May. If she had a problem, she would ask Paul to help. He met the Governor on occasion, but to the politician, Paul was just another inmate.

Paul remembers one exchange with the Governor. Paul had made Gravlax, a Nordic dish consisting of salmon that is cured using rock salt.

The Governor told him, "You know, you make the best Gravlax that I've ever eaten."

Paul was impressed with himself until he overheard that the Governor said the same thing to another inmate three months later.

The good times during those hours at the Governor's Mansion didn't last for the entirety of his prison stay. During one dinner rush, a hefty guard was walking around and whether intentional or not, got in the way of the busy inmates. Paul ran into him and muttered, "Hey man, you got to get out of the way."

The guard was instantly offended. He looked at Paul and said with rage, "Boy, who are you talking to?"

Paul acknowledged the error and cowed back to his chore. Later that day Paul replayed the incident to Miss May.

Rather than dismiss the confrontation, Miss May yelled to the Guard in front of all the kitchen staff, "Get your ass in there and sit on that stool."

The anger flashed in his eyes.

Two months later, as Paul was nearing closer to his discharge date, he had another run in with that guard.

At the time Paul was serving time in a unit where he could jog the perimeter daily. A tower overlooks the yard, and that same man that Paul had blown the whistle on stood watch, looking down at Paul.

The resentful guard calls down and tells the other guard that Paul Dysart just threatened him.

That's one of the ten big sins in prison, explained Paul, "That's 'in the hole' time. I was immediately placed in cuffs and marched to the hole where my privileges were stripped from me and my release date was extended for another year."

"You have no idea how it is to lose that date," Paul remembers solemnly.

As Paul lay in bed in the hole, he re-read "Mutiny on the Bounty."

Paul said, "I remembered how that guy got out of it by telling it like it was — so I wrote a letter to my girlfriend in Sioux Falls, and I asked her to pass it on to Miss May."

Back in Sioux Falls, Katie received the letter that explained that the guard that accused Paul of threatening him was the same guard that held a grudge all because of an innocent, "you're in the way" comment. Katie forwarded the letter on to the Governor's Mansion in care of Miss May as Paul had asked her to.

Even though the Mansion didn't get involved with internal prison matters, Paul was relieved when Miss May pulled some kind of an act that caused his case to be re-examined.

With a few witnesses, including two other guards, Paul was able to convince the Board that the accusation of the guard was just a retaliatory act. Paul was released from the hole and his new release date was granted — Jan. 15, 1985.

Paul's advice, "The main thing to understand about life inside a prison is that it is life at a different level, where if you just do your time, one day at a time with blinders on you can handle it without issues."

The release day will forever be etched in his memory. Paul left the Missouri State Penitentiary and got a bus ticket to Kansas City, where Katie picked him up.

"The second thing I wanted to do was put my suitcase down," Paul laughs as he recalls the day.

The happiness found was short lived. While in prison, Katie had fallen in love with another man and she was battling that, someone had told Paul. He knew that possibility existed, he knew he was the one that got locked up and didn't hold her choices against her.

"The guy has a nice job and a car and what do I have?" Paul questioned everything.

But rather than feel dejected, he immediately started to look for work.

Paul was over 40, still a Black man and now an ex-convict, which made the job search daunting. So instead of waiting for the lucky break, he created his own. That summer he borrowed his brother's truck and started a concrete company.

An important life lesson: When the cards aren't there play your own game.

Building & Rebuilding a Family (ongoing)

At 23 and married and learning how to be the decision making adult following decisions made by first, mom, then a sergeant/officer, now a wife. Paul attempted to have it all — working at the Post Office, playing Y basketball, fastpitch softball, and hanging out with the team more than being a father to his Tracy, Paul, Sherry and Yolanda. His wife, Brenda and he discovered that they were more like a brother/sister act and divorced after eight years.

Then there was Leslie, and her exceptional Rensburger family the next eight years, followed by Katie, Heather and Danny Merrill for the following eight years. Throw in Melody Hoff and her special Jennifer, Barbara, Gary, DJ, and Brice. All of whom got a small taste of family importance.

Putting up with Paul through three pregnancies and two children during the late 70s, Pam Nugteren decided to marry Leroy Rodgers in 1984. That union wasn't working out when Paul was released from prison in January 15, 1985.

By September, as she worked nights at the local VFW, she was in need of a babysitter. On September 1, 1985 Paul decided to get to know these two kids of his and moved in to help out. By 1987 to help with all the confusion as there were two Nugteren's, one Rodgers and one Dysart, he decided to get their names changed, which he knew meant he was in the commitment for the long haul.

He says, "It looks like Pam is in it for the long haul, too, as we are still sticking our feet under the same sheets and table."

Their commitment remains, and Tracy, Paul, Nicole Annette, Sherry, Yolanda, Nicole Lynn, and Tamien have produced 17 Grands, and as of Sept 23, 2020, 12 Great Grands.

"With that in mind, God has been good to me! More so than I deserve," Paul reflects with a smile.

Paul credits Nicole and Tamien for finally teaching him to be a family man. During his first stint as President of the local NAACP he got his first taste at what was to come.

Paul organized a picnic at the McKennan Park where he convinced Ernie into securing a vehicle to be used as the winning prize in a drawing. With his mother, Lettie Mae, in attendance among the roughly 150 festive partiers, this feisty little three year old girl loudly proclaimed, "That's my daddy!"

Unbeknownst to Lettie that this was one of her grandchildren, she proclaimed right back to the beautiful little child, "You don't say?"

As if to say, "tell me more." Which was how Nicole, Tamien, and their mom, Pam Nugteren met Lettie Mae.

Working at various jobs since high school in Monroe, Marion, and Parker, SD, Pam found herself in need of a babysitter as she worked the night shift. From day one, Nicole and Tamien began their training sessions on Paul's "Family Man" course.

One session occurred as Paul was going to take Nicole's car keys from her. He grabbed her by the shoulder, twisted her and sat her down on the bed. Before Paul realized what was happening, she sprung up, twisted his shoulder, and sat him down. By the time Nicole was finished, not only did she keep the keys, but she got $20 for gas.

Prior to her driving days both of the kids had Pam and Paul following the soccer scene. Tamien was a pretty good goalie.

One memory that stands out for Paul was Tamien's solicitation of permission to get his ear pierced, Paul saw it as his first expression of public acknowledgement.

Another giant step in Tamien's training for Paul, came as he was disrespecting his mom and she called Paul.

"When I pulled up to our house," Paul remembers, "there were two cop cars there because when Pam told him his dad was on his way home, he called the police. After a few tense moments, and the exit of the police, all electronic devices were boxed up and removed from his room for about five weeks."

Once the electronics were off-limits Tamien began to devour reading.

Nicole was all over the soccer scene through the years. A program called, Dakota Gold, mainly led by Gary Karl and John Goodale, provided way more than the family's share of tournament victories from Minneapolis, MN, to Omaha, NE to Kansas City, KS to Denver, CO. From Nicole's goalie beginning, thru 13 years as assistant soccer coach at Paul's Alma (St. Joseph Cathedral) O'Gorman High School, Nicole Nugteren-Dysart-Zacher has provided more entertainment and education than anyone could possibly ask for.

Paul knows that race has been an issue for the 79 years he's been alive, because of that, it has dictated that he stress to his children that they are not to accept being called the N word, as that is the first punch in a fight.

"Don't you know," Paul recalls, "It was fifth grade when Nicole was tested that way, and she responded just as I had instructed. The parents of the girl who took the ass whooping took us to court. I explained to the judge that I strongly teach my children that no one has the right to degrade you like that, and the N-word is the first punch in a fight. A little probation was granted as the training continued."

September 1, 1985 is a date that Paul holds dear.

"I moved into a house as a 44 year old and was luckily taught how to pitch in and make it a home," He says, "Here 35 plus years later the training continues!"

Building a Business (1985)

Upon returning to Sioux Falls after the year and a half of the "war on drugs sentence" in Jefferson City, Mo., being over 40, still Black, and now an ex-con, landing a job proved challenging.

Pouring concrete was something Paul had learned in the Seabees. So he borrowed a pick-up and got a few concrete tools and started The Dysart Company, a concrete company. Paul set out to make a name for himself. Once he started getting jobs, he began to hire employees. Paul made it a point to hire Native Americans, ex-convicts, and those that other businesses deemed "un-hire-able." He knew what it felt like to be on the other side of the desk.

It worked for him; at the peak of his business he had 55 employees. Other big companies in the industry still seemed to get first pick for the jobs, and all of the state contracts. Paul's employees, too, would jump ship to the larger companies when things got slow. Paul became a training ground of sorts, the big companies would see the work the men did and feel more confident giving them a chance with their operations.

"We were the last to be called and the first ones to be let go," Paul said.

One day that stands out in Paul's memory was around 1995 or 1996. He and his crew were doing spall repair out in Pierre on the hottest day not only in the state of South Dakota, but the entire country.

Spalling concrete refers to concrete that has become pitted, flaked, or broken up. It is repaired by removing the damaged section so that it can be filled with cement.

Paul's ingenuity was evident to his crew, and his work ethic was never questioned. Even as the boss, he was fine doing heaving lifting.

The heat was stifling. Some men would work on the road, as Paul stood on the trailer. He had it rigged up so the gravel, sand and 100 pound bags of concrete and mixer were up on the trailer, along with a big trough of water. Paul would hoist the bags up on his shoulder and drop them in to the water to mix it. Two other guys ran the weiler broom.

It was one right after another, Paul added ice to the water. It was so damn hot, he would reach into the water and wipe his face, not realizing that he was getting concrete poisoning.

The state shut down the work around 2 p.m. that day due to the extreme heat. So the entire crew headed back to town.

The next morning, Paul awoke puffed up like his pores

couldn't breathe. Paul waited it out, and within a day or so was back to normal. Lesson learned.

Paul said, "I had an opportunity to make a dent, getting work I mean. But prejudice is in a different form. It's economic. We have a chance to drink at the same container as you, and share food with you, but it's economically a rigged system. It's about race."

As one of five Black contractors out of Sioux Falls Paul said they made attempts to be included in the various Department of Transportation (DOT) Minority Business Enterprise (MBE) Contracts to level the playing field on the dollars the Federal Government passed back to the states for infrastructure work. By giving the 10% GOAL money that was marked for MBE's to white contractors that either claimed a percentage of Native American blood, or put the business in their wife's name, becoming a woman owned business, thus now putting women which were 51% of the U.S. population, along with another roughly 20% of non-white people in a pool — all now competing for that 10% of the DOT contracts awarded on its infastructure projects. An article in the Sioux Falls SD Argus Leader on Monday March 20, 1995 regarding the Affirmative Action Controversy in the State, is one of many articles the Argus has reported on with very, very little success in moving the needle towards real efforts at leveling the playing field leading to inclusion by legitimate Minority Businesses.

The state was able to convince the Federal Government that they were in compliance with the DOT guidelines by awarding over half a billion dollars worth of contracts to these phony companies, while bankrupting four of the five Black contractors thru the late 80s to the early 2000s.

Paul explains how his company ended up, "On April 23, 1991, my lawyer, Dennis McFarland, was able to put the company debts in the hands of the white partner and he and the bank each gave me $20,000.00 to move on, and not to sue.

Copies of the two $20,000 checks given to Paul to start over without his line of credit, and the agreement that he wouldn't sue.

Paul has documented his long work history with all of the business cards that he has carried over the years.

Without a bank, and being labeled too committed to holding the state complicit for its failure in support for real and obvious minorities, the concrete part of the business slowly became untenable and evolved into mainly sealing paved streets and highways."

The thought of carrying out the family business with his son came to a halt in August 1998; while finishing up sealing a street in Yankton, SD, Paul's youngest boy (then 19) bypassed a shutdown procedure and hot tar shot out — scalding the upper right portion of his arm and chest. Paul remembers visiting him in the hospital.

"He looked at me and said, 'Dad this ain't it'. He went on to get his business degree and is doing just great," Paul says.

Within a couple years, the removal of a disk and fusion of two vertebrae in 1965, Paul's back wouldn't take any more upright work, so the construction field had to be put in the rear view mirror for The Dysart Co /TDC INC /and PED INC.

Paul took on a white partner and was extended a better line of credit. He thought nothing of the situation until he realized as he was working his ass off, the white partner was using his Blackness to get the contracts. So Paul changed things up and made it so that only he was able to sign the checks. The next day, the bank called his credit due. A settlement followed, but the whole situation left a sour taste in his mouth.

He later did reach out to lawyer Gerry Spence, with a letter written in 1997.

Letter to lawyer Gerry Spence, written in 1997:

To Whom it may concern:

Let me introduce myself as Paul E. Dysart, Sr. a Black American born in Atchison, KS, Sept. 23, 1940 whose family of mom, dad and three siblings moved to Sioux Falls, SD in 1946. I was educated by the Dominican nuns as the first Black family to attend St. Joseph Cathedral in this town of 50,000 people. Now the population is around 120,000. After high school in 1958, as all my white classmates melted into society, I was all of a sudden a Black man. Which was mild as to what I was referred to. I enlisted in the US Army, received my honorable discharge and returned home where I had the choice of four Black girls to marry in 1962. I married the preacher's daughter and we have three beautiful children from the marriage that lasted eight years.

After being denied the opportunity of becoming the first Black law enforcement officer in this State, because I was told, "you have too many shady relatives." I was hired as the token Black for our local Post Office for six years. After being denied a loan from our Credit Union because of my fierce stand as union steward and Vice President of the union, I was told to reapply for the loan by the supervisor, that denied it the first time, now things seemed to be going smoothly. I left and was hired as the token Black for the local IBM (I've Been Moved) as a customer engineer. After six years I wanted to go into sales as a few of my classmates were making better money. I was told by management that Black people couldn't sell in this part of the country.

So I left them and became a Black Gypsy driving an old covered school bus to Mexico and bringing back pottery, leather goods, etc. One of the large department stores saw the little success we were having and started sending semi trucks down down there so we were out of business.

While recovering from back surgery in 1976, I drove down to Kansas City to visit a sister, and was arrested for possession of 32 "hits" of speed and given a five year suspended imposition of sentence because it is the first time I had been in any trouble with the law. Race is an issue.

Back home, I took advantage of a personal relationship to contact a wealthy relative living in San Diego who owned a considerable parcel of land directly in the growth plan of this town. He gave me the consent to proceed in getting an architect and realtor involved. I did both and was told by the realtor that I would receive commissions on the lots sold if I could pass the Real Estate exam. I became the first Black

Realtor in the state of SD. When I presented my license to the land owner, he informed me that he could not hire me because I had too many debts. This Zealot has used that land development to leverage himself into the top Real Estate Broker in the state. Race is an issue.

After walking four and half years of my suspended sentence from Kansas City down with no contact with the law, my landlord was busted for the sale of marijuana. His choices were to bite the bullet and do the time or set up people. Because we were "friends" and had partied on numerous occasions, he knew I could find some cocaine. During the late seventies and early eighties, it was the "in" thing to do some drugs while partying. It was common knowledge that several city officials were doing the same thing. At the time, I was raising my two oldest children and working three jobs, and was the President of the local NAACP. After making some calls I found someone that had what my landlord wanted. He sent "a friend" over to get the drugs from me because this friend didn't trust anyone. After that first encounter, the record shows they called me twenty-five times in the next thirty days trying to get them all kinds of drugs. I succumbed on three occasions. Then when I just refused to be involved any longer, they busted me and gave me three years for the sale of cocaine. I was offered the same "deal" that my landlord was given. Because I hung around the skunk, I stunk, so I refused to give anybody up. I served one year here in South Dakota and was transported to Missouri where I had to do one and one half years of the suspended sentence. Race is an issue.

I returned home January 25, 1985 to attempt to put my life back together. After working in the kitchen of the Governor's Mansion in Missouri and cooking for Governor Kit Bond for about eight months, I applied for a fry cook job that was advertised in our local paper. I was denied the job because I was over 40, still Black, and now an ex con.

People asked me why I don't just leave and start over someplace else. My answer has always been, someplace else I am what I am. An over 40, Black ex-con and if one cannot make it at home, where you are known, then where? Race is an issue.

After having doors closed in my face, I decided to start my own business. I borrowed my brothers pickup truck and some concrete tools and started doing sidewalks and other concrete flatwork. From 1985 to 1987, I made modest progress. Then one of the bigger white contractors summoned me and said he was going to make me a star. We started a Corporation that I was made President of and finally, I was bidding on and "helping" oversee contracts in excess of a half million dollars. It should have been the best of times. In 1990, I finally realized what the golden rule was all about. He had the gold, so he ruled. He didn't pay the taxes and only paid enough bills to barely keep us going. His intent was to push my company into bankruptcy and let me swing in the wind.

I contacted a lawyer that was able to help because the day after I went to the bank to state no one but me would sign checks, the bank sent me a certified letter calling my loan due. My lawyer was able to put the bills where they belonged and the bank and this contractor each gave me $20,000 not to sue them. I took the money and tried to start over.

During my years in the construction field, I personally trained hundreds of Black, Native Americans, and ex-convicts that were previously thought of as unemployable, many of them are now good tax paying employees for those same firms that wouldn't give them an initial chance. Race is an issue.

Now enter the Government (SBA). I went to them for a loan to help me get back into the game. They gave me a $150,000 equipment loan in 1991 and not a penny for operating capital. They accepted me into their 8(a) program and required me to send them a quarterly report of my finances. With this financial information they always knew where my company stood. While they were finding and presenting blue-eyed Native Americans and wealthy white women, wives of successful contractors, with contracts from $10,000 to in excess of a million dollars, they helped me get about $50,000 total over a period of five years. I still have a *copy of the document they signed stating that they were going to get me $100,000 the first year through $500,000 the fifth year.*

One of the Government's (SBA) best success stories is the story of a white contractor with a Vietnamese wife that speaks and understands little English, but owns 51% of their company was presented a million dollar contract they completed in less than nine months for a profit in excess of $300,000. While the SBA gave me the equipment loan and the "indication" they were going to assist me as they did for minority and non-minority people, it was a cruel hoax. I never asked them to do the work for me, only do for me what they mislead me to believe they were going to do. Although the quality of my work was never called into question, the level playing field did not exist. Race is an issue.

The final straw came in 1995 when I went to the local VA hospital to ask for the contract to remove their incinerator. I then went to the SBA to ask them to make it an 8(a) contract, which they did for about $25,000. I completed the job only to have the Government (SBA) tell the Government (VA) to give them the money. I never saw one dime of the contract money. Shortly thereafter, the SBA came and picked up all of my equipment and put it on auction. To this day, I don't know how much the sale was worth. I was told by the Government (SBA) to file for bankruptcy to put the matter behind me.

Also, to this day I am hounded by the vendors on the VA project for their money. Race is an issue.

I have documentation for all of the above, but in South Dakota, as a Black man, you can't get lawyers to sue because good 'ole boys don't sue good 'ole boys. I wrote my Senators Daschle and Pressler and Congressman Johnson. Nothing! Good 'ole boys don't go after good 'ole boys. I finally wrote Representatives Charlie Rangle and Maxine Waters but you know what that means, good 'ole Government people cover for good 'ole Government people when it comes to good 'ole Government. So, been there and done that. Race is an issue.

On this one year anniversary of the Gerry Spence (American Trial Lawyer) article in the April 1996 issue of Playboy I remember you made me feel like you really give a damn. You said, "In fact, you begin to feel like a Black man. I feel like a Black man. People will misunderstand that. I feel as if I have been banished along with the poor and the damned and the injured and the forgotten and the hated. They are my clients. If you live with them and suffer with them and care about them and love them every day of your life, you begin to understand."

The Government, from my Senators and Representative, to the SBA to the VA, has made me feel the powerlessness. Their own records will prove all l that I have stated and they *are fearless in doing what they have done to me because <u>race is an issue</u>.*

I'm not just a whining, drug dealing, Black man out here in South Dakota that has taken and taken. My record also shows I was president of the local NAACP, Vice President of the Postal Clerks Union, ten year coach for boys and girls at the YMCA, usher at the Catholic Church, driver for Meals on Wheels, member of a Kiwanis Club that mentors students, and an Advisory Board member at our local Salvation Army.

I believe I have a case regarding my Government. As a life member of the Disabled American Veterans, I believe they done me wrong. Just because these good 'ole boys won't sue the other good 'ole boys, would you consider it?

Sincerely,
Paul E. Dysart, Sr.

Pardons (2003)

When Paul turned 62 he was ready to stop the heavy lifting and find a job that didn't tax his body so. Options such as driving bus for the local school district or getting involved in non-profit work never seemed possible because of his criminal record, it was as though he was always ineligible for the job.

To rectify the situation, Paul sought the support, of then South Dakota Governor, Bill Janklow. Paul sent Governor Janklow a letter, dated January 2, 2003. In less than 24-hours a pardon was officially granted by the State of South Dakota from the Governor dated Jan 3, 2003.

Now that the felony was no longer in the way, Paul went on to drive bus within several school districts until his retirement in 2017. He drove five years for the Sioux Falls School District and five years for the Tea Area School District. During his bus driving days, Paul found ways to share his wisdom with the youth that filled his seats.

Twice, Paul wore a dashiki to work, just so the children would ask him about it.

The first time was to honor President Barack Obama's first day in the Oval Office. Obama was inaugurated on January 20, 2009, elected as the 44th U.S. president, and the first African American president elected to the White House.

Paul was driving bus in the Sioux Falls School District at the time. The blue dashiki was special to Paul because it came from President Obama's grandmother's village in Kenya. Years prior, Paul's daughter was able to visit the village and brought several colorful garments back for her father.

"I am a very proud Black man that has lived in South Dakota since 1946. This was to show my pride in the first African American president; and because I am a bus driver, it's about education. The students learn something from it," Paul said.

He did the same thing eight years later, wearing a dashiki to drive school kids on President Obama's last day in office in 2017.

"We need conversations," Paul said in a local newspaper interview about it. "We're going to miss him. Michelle, Barack, their two girls and mother-in-law — we had class in our White House. I'm proud of what he has done. It's my little shout out to them."

The newspaper article ran the same year Paul retired from driving bus.

Paul's later years have been filled with good things — love, kids, grandkids, and friendship.

"I've had a good life," Paul said, "Even through all the hard times. I've been duly wronged but that's why I got that pardon in less than 24 hours; because they know. I get all beamed up because I get to see my grand-babies now, despite it all, I'm blessed on the other end. I got to live this kind of the life thanks to those who came before me. Life is just a bowl a cherries. Why can't we all just get along?"

Paul E. Dysart, SR.
940 Kevin Drive
Tea, SD 57064

January 2, 2003

Governor Bill Janklow,

I could fill this correspondence with all kinds of stories of my involvement in all kinds of stories. Instead, I would like to cut to the chase and simply say that I would like you to consider granting me a pardon for my involvement in some of those stories twenty plus years ago. Since being released from incarceration Jan 15, 1985, I have, for the most part, been forced to be self employed. After applying for advertised positions, it was basically said that I need not apply because I was over forty, black, and an ex con.

I fast forward to November 2002, and was denied an opportunity to compete with my son at Household Credit Services here in what I consider my hometown. Because 20 years ago, I became a two time felon for (1) possession of 34 hits of white crosses and (2) sale of cocaine, even though the record should show contact always coming from the people that busted me. I did plea guilty of the charges brought against me because I was guilty as charged.

Since Jan. 15 1985, I have been self employed as a concrete contractor. I have pulled my stints as a driver for wheels on meals, coached kids for the YMCA & YWCA, was an advisory board member for the Salvation Army, and still a volunteer driver for the VA Hospital on Wednesday mornings.

After going to the Country of Botswana, which is a landlocked Country in sub-Saharan Africa, as South Dakota is a landlocked State here in our Country, on two occasions and visiting with people there about the possibility and feasibility of wiring their schools like you did here in this State, I could use some help, guidance, and council with this project. My felony problems get in the way.

Assisting my sister at Marie's Workroom with negotiations and exploratory possibilities with Larry Manderscheid, VP Sales & Marketing at Aerostar, and George Eagleman of the United Sioux Tribes, teaching both native Americans and the new immigrants from South America and Africa, sewing classes, with an eye on the hope of securing some contracts that will create a win win situation for a group of people that are eager to use this avenue as one way of helping ease themselves into this strange new environment. My felony problems seem to get in the way.

One more attempt was made to join a tele-marketing firm and a question rose its ugly head and my stupidity of twenty plus years ago still get in the way. I am now over sixty, still am black, and still an ex-con. Whatever time I have left on this earth, I would like for you to eliminate that problem from the equation. Would you please consider my personal request?

Sincerely,
Paul E. Dysart, Sr.

JAN. 2, 2003 - THE LETTER PAUL WROTE TO GOVERNOR BILL JANKLOW.

State of South Dakota

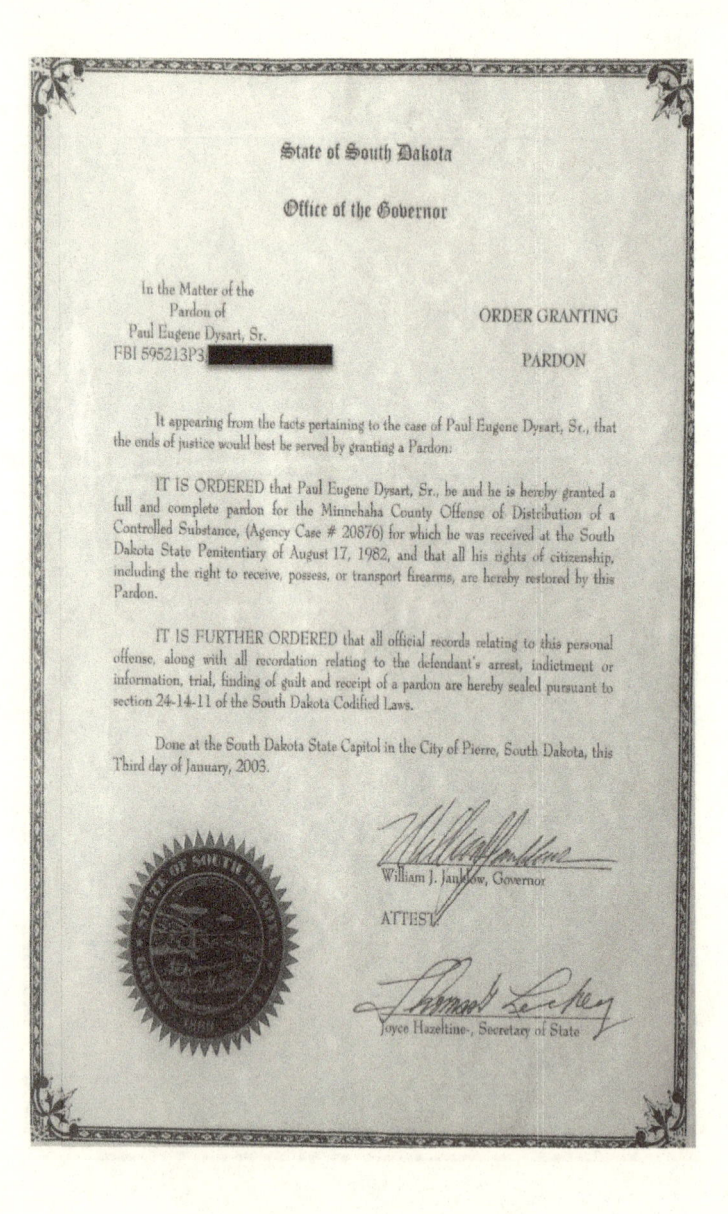

Office of the Governor

In the Matter of the
Pardon of
Paul Eugene Dysart, Sr.
FBI 595213P3,

ORDER GRANTING

PARDON

It appearing from the facts pertaining to the case of Paul Eugene Dysart, Sr., that the ends of justice would best be served by granting a Pardon:

IT IS ORDERED that Paul Eugene Dysart, Sr., be and he is hereby granted a full and complete pardon for the Minnehaha County Offense of Distribution of a Controlled Substance, (Agency Case # 20876) for which he was received at the South Dakota State Penitentiary of August 17, 1982, and that all his rights of citizenship, including the right to receive, possess, or transport firearms, are hereby restored by this Pardon.

IT IS FURTHER ORDERED that all official records relating to this personal offense, along with all recordation relating to the defendant's arrest, indictment or information, trial, finding of guilt and receipt of a pardon are hereby sealed pursuant to section 24-14-11 of the South Dakota Codified Laws.

Done at the South Dakota State Capitol in the City of Pierre, South Dakota, this Third day of January, 2003.

William J. Janklow, Governor

ATTEST:

Joyce Hazeltine, Secretary of State

**IN LESS THAN 24 HOURS
PAUL WAS GRANTED A PARDON.**

Dysart's Just Right BBQ Sauce

One dream that is still in the works to this day, 2020, is Paul's BBQ sauce. Dysart's of the Dakota's BBQ Sauce is something Paul is very proud of, and he hopes to make into a business someday. He is reaching out to his friends and family in various cities in the U.S. to plan gatherings with his nine year military brothers and sisters, his Catholic brothers and sisters, his Irish cousins, and his African cousins, to show we can all get along.

His secret sauce recipe, passed down from generation to generation, is currently bottled up in plastic Sunkist and Mountain Dew soda bottles that Paul hands out to friends and family. With that bottle of the "just right" meat sauce he includes a small slip of paper, one that sums up his story of how the sauce came to be.

It reads: Joseph Dysart was born in Ballyhallen, Donegel-Ulster Ireland and died in 1731. Joseph had three sons, all born in Ireland. Captain Johnson John Dysart was one of his sons, and was an officer in the War of 1812, as well as a plantation owner. Captain Johnston John Dysart and an unknown Black woman on his plantation had three children: America, Finly and Lemuel Dysart. Finly Dysart was born in 1815 in Rockcastle County, Kentucky. His race is listed as Mulatto/Black. His son Finly J. Dysart was born in 1858 in Buchanan County, Missouri. His race is listed as Black. Finly died in 1915 in Atchison, Kansas. Finly J's son. Lawrence Matthew Dyasrt, born in 1895 in Atchison, Kansas, died in 1945. Lawrence Matthew Dysart had a son, Lawrence Alexander Dysart, who was born in 1915 in Atchison, Kansas and died in Sioux Falls, South Dakota in 1968.

Lawrence A's son Paul E Dysart was born in 1940 in Atchison, Kansas and moved with brother Lawrence A Dysart, Jr. , Doris Dysart, Marie Dysart, and Johnetta Dysart to Sioux Falls, South Dakota in 1946. Additional children born to the family were: Robert Dysart, Cathy Dysart, Carlotta Dysart, and Rita Dysart.

When great great grandad Finley left Kentucky after being freed as a slave, he grabbed the "sauce" recipe from the big house and began making it for family and friends. The recipe has been personally handed to Finley J. Dysart to Lawrence M Dysart, to Lawrence A. Dysart and before he went blind in 1964, he gave the recipe and story to Paul E. Dysart Sr., who has been mixing and making it for over 50 years.

Written by Paul E. Dysart, Sr.
June 2020:

From Emmett Till to Black Lives Matter

Almost 80 and coming this far in this Black skin in the midst of the pandemic and the Black Lives Matter movement saying, enough, enough, enough. The numbers of the white robe wearing power brokers are dwindling and the millennials plus have taken to the streets around the world. From our country coming to grips with THE ORIGINAL SIN (slavery) while taking the country from the Native inhabitants and allowing the original slave hunters to evolve into what is the present day police force, thankfully the children and grandchildren of that dwindling number is what seems to give a glimmer of hope — that the United States of America will finally become that shining city on the hill.

At the same age as Emmett Till in 1955, I lived under the umbrella of the Catholic Church of St. Joseph Cathedral in Sioux Falls SD. Emmett lived in Chicago and was visiting a relative in Money, Mississippi. A white lady told her husband that this 14 year old boy whistled at her, a charge she admitted she had lied about 63 years later. The husband and a cousin beat and hung Emmett so bad that his Mother insisted an open casket for his funeral, so the world could see what they did to her boy. It made world news. At that point I realized outside this Catholic umbrella, life was different. God love the Dominican nuns that took me through 12 years and silently ingrained the education of any other privileged Catholic kid.

Fast forward to 1959, as a private in the US Army, in Fort Ord, CA, getting hit in the mouth by another Black soldier for having a picture of a white girl in my wallet. Just believe it, he got his and I'll leave it there. Next, in 1959 while stationed with KMAG in Wonju' Korea, won the region championship in basketball and was then in 1960 stationed at Ft. Devens, MA where I was the luckiest guy to be there with some terrific basketball players and we won the first Army Championship over Ft. Dix, NJ, the perennial champions. I was fortunate enough that year to compete against two Hall of Famers, Lenny Wilkins and John Thompson. For winning the championship, the base Commander sent us on a tour through DC, VA, and the Carolinas. While riding the bus through NC, we stopped to have lunch in our uniforms at a cafe. There were four other Black players on our team who were all from the South so I thought nothing of them getting to the door and opening it for me. As the first inside the cafe, people actually dropped silverware as their mouths opened. I stepped right up to the counter and sat down. The other Black soldiers went right to the restroom and stayed until the Captain called the manager out to say, we are the US ARMY and we all are here to eat. All the kitchen help was Black and I know our helpings reflected that. As we were leaving after our meal, once outside they showed me the sign on the door that these 20 year old eyes saw for the first time ever! "NO N****RS OR DOGS ALLOWED".

Getting honorably discharged in 1962 I returned to Sioux Falls where there were four Black girls that were available for me to court. So in 1962 I married the Baptist preacher's daughter.

From the moment I arrived back to Sioux Falls, the social scene consisted of bars that were western music driven and the only accepted Black person that was made comfortable in their presence was Charlie Pride. Many physical confrontations happened simply because a white girl dare ask any of us Black guys to dance.

During the Motown and Disco era. and our Red Willow and Myron Lee live performances, one bar, the Macomba Club, made the move after the demise of Shorty's Club and turned on the music, created the atmosphere, and became THE place to go. Despite the success, the white owners were uncomfortable with all the interracial dancing so they switched to playing western music. The Black patrons went across the street to frequent Earl's, a great disco. The ones who liked to dance joined us for many months of dancing and partying until two Black guys got into a physical confrontation and the owner lost it and barred ALL Black guys.

One block away sat Shannon O'Neills. Being hip to our lip, O'Neills began playing the music and the crowds gathered there until once again, that race thing reared its ugly head and the owners believed the way to put a stop to this interracial dancing was to turn on the western music.

Recognizing what the faithful customers wanted, the Macomba Club became Nite City and the gang recycled back. The above social scene experience took place in a one block area of downtown Sioux Falls, SD over about a ten year period. Because race is an issue and there were nine (9) of us Black children in the Dysart family, we all can testify that indeed Black Lives Matter. Not to the detriment of any other Lives. Inclusion on a level playing field isn't too much to ask for our grandchildren to be a part of.

Extras & Snapshots

Current River Sheetcake

1 cup butter

1/2 cup cocoa

1 cup water

2 cups sugar

2 cups flour, unsifted

1 teaspoon baking soda

2 eggs, slightly beaten

1/2 cup cup sour cream or buttermilk

2 teaspoons vanilla extract

Chocolate Nut icing

1/2 cup butter

1/4 cup cocoa

6 tablespoons evaporated milk

16 ounce box confectioners' sugar

1 cup chopped nuts

1 teaspoon vanilla extract

Preheat oven to 350°

Grease 15.5 x 10.5 inch Jelly Roll pan well.

Combine butter, cocoa and water in a saucepan, bring to a full boil. While still hot, pour mixture over combined sugar, flour and baking soda, mix well. Add eggs sour cream (buttermilk) and vanilla, mix well. Pour batter into pan, bake 15 minutes. Do not overtake. While cake is baking, make the icing. Ice cake immediately after removing from one.

Mix butter, cocoa, and milk in a saucepan until boiling point. Add confectioners' sugar, nuts, and vanilla, mix well. Additional milk may be added to make icing more spreadable.

20-24 serving.

A sinfully rich and easy dessert. So named because it always packed in the cooler for our annual spring float trip on Currant River.

From, "Past & Repast; the history and hospitality of the Missouri Governor's Mansion" — Copyright 1983.

Tamien's daily prayer for his dad

GOD open my eyes to the wonderful truths of your instructions. I can do all things thru Christ who gives me all the strength I need. If GOD is with us, who can be against us? I expect great things to come to fruition in my life and through my life. I shall show the potential of possibilities. I AM HEALTHY, VIBRANT, AND FULL OF LIFE!!!

Paul suggests you repeat this 10 times per day until it becomes ingrained.

Below: Paul's dad, Lawrence A (Scoop) Dysart with entertainer Duke Ellington taken in 1952 at the old Sioux Falls airport restaurant.

Dysart's of the Dakota's BBQ Sauce

Joseph Dysart was born in Ballyhallen, Donegal-Ulster Ireland and died in 1731. Joseph had 3 sons, all born in Ireland. Captain Johnston John Dysart was one of his sons and an Officer of War in 1812. He was also a plantation owner. Captain Johnston John Dysart and unknown black women had 3 children – America, Finly and Lemuel Dysart.

Finly Dysart was born in 1815 in Rockcastle County, Kentucky; his race is listed as Mulatto/Black. He had a son Finley J. Dysart who was born in 1858 in Buchanan County, Missouri, his race was listed as Black. Finley J. died in 1915 in Atchison Kansas. Finley J had a son, Lawrence Matthew Dysart, born in 1895 in Atchison Kansas, died in 1945. Lawrence M. had a son Lawrence Alexander who was born in 1915 in Atchison Kansas and died in Sioux Falls SD in 1968.

Lawrence A's son Paul E. Dysart was born in 1940 in Atchison Kansas and moved with brother Lawrence A. Jr., Doris, Marie and Johnetta Dysart to Sioux Falls SD in 1946. Additional children born to the family were: Robert A. Dysart 1948, Cathy Dysart 1949, Carlotta Dysart 1950 and Rita Dysart 1951.

When great-great granddad Finly left Kentucky after being freed as a slave he grabbed the "sauce" recipe from the big house and began making it for family and friends. The recipe has been personally handed to Finley J. Dysart to Lawrence M. Dysart to Lawrence A. Dysart and before he went blind in 1964, he gave the story and recipe to Paul E. Dysart, Sr. who has been mixing and making it for over 50 years.

Cathedral High School: Won the Trophy in 1958

Paul and Joan Lalley at the Press Ball '58

Above: 1958 - Entered the Army
Below: 1964 – 70 Navy Seabees

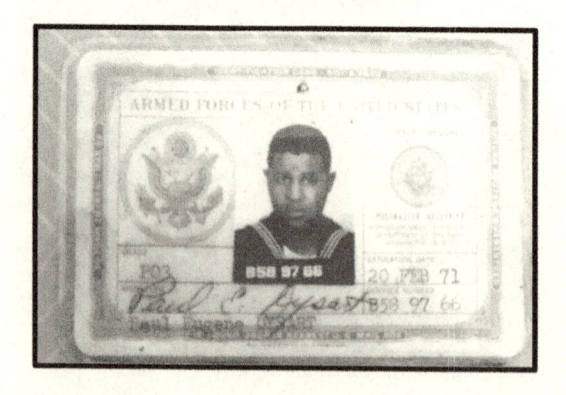

Grandma Lettie and FX with the crew
during Paul's Hippie years.

Did I say Hippie Years!!!
Paul with Brenda, Tracy, Paul, Sherry and Yoki.

Paul photographed with Jessie Jackson when he came to Sioux Falls to speak during his presidential run.

Paul shaking hands with Mr. Naftely, owner of top security firm in South Africa.

Trip to Botswana in 1988

Paul driving school bus, wearing his Dashiki from Kenya commemorating President Obama inauguration in 2008.

Above: FX…always a Twins Fan!

Below: Oldest Brother Lloyd in Mpls with Marie & Larry,

The babies, daughter Nicole, son Tamien and Pam.

Paul's first taste of the stage!

Paul later preformed in To Kill a Mocking Bird
and of Mice and Men

Above: A wonderful visit from grandsons with India ties - Clay, Cedric and Cade Kamaleson. Also pictured are the SF grandkids Destiny, Tyreese, Mekhi and Saniya.

Below: Oldest grandson Dorian Craig.

The Siblings!

Above: Marie, (FX), Johnetta, Carlotta, Paul, Cathy and (Jaden).
Below: Paul, Johnetta, Carlotta, Rita, Marie and Bobby.

Bobby, Carlotta, Rita, Paul and Cathy celebrating Johnetta's life

Paul pictured with nephew Brent Dysart

Above: Trip to Chicago to visit daughter Nicole Annette and the boys. Cade, Pam, Paul, Cedric and Nicole (not pictured is Clay)

Below: Nicole Annette and Paul

Paul and Michael Dysart with Carlotta and Mark Willard during Paul's 75th birthday celebration

Paul and sister Johnetta Dysart

Visit to Denver: Pictured are sons Tamien and Paul Jr. and daughters Sherry and Yoki.

Five of Paul's kids: Sherry, Yoki, Paul Jr., Nicole Annette and Tracy

A 75th Birthday Celebration surrounded by kids and grandkids.

Good friends, Char Swenson-Poncelet and husband Paul

Paul and Pam!

Trip to Denver 2020

Above: Grandsons Xavier and SirDevon.

Below: Daughter's Yoki and Sherry with grandkids Xavier, Kyndra, Chelsae and great-grand kids.

Above: Son Jr. Paul with grandson Nathan and great-grandson Ezekiel.

Below: Grandkids SirDevon and Trinity Dysart.

Christmas 2020: Paul and Pam pictured with grandkids Tyreese, Saniya, Amira, Destiny and Mekhi.

Great-grandbabies Lamon'e and Harmon'e

Daughter
Tracy Dysart
and her sons
Dorian and
Brent

Daughter-in-Law
**Charlene
Salgado -Dysart**
and her kids
SirDevon and
Trinity
(son Paul Jr.)

Daughters **Yolanda & Sherry Dysart** and her kids Xavier, Chelsae, Kyndra

Daughter **Nicole Kamaleson** and her son's Clay, Cedric and Cade

Daughter **Nicole Zacher**
and her kids Tyreese and Mekhi (husband Mike)

Son Tamien Dysart
and his daughter's Destiny, Amira, Saniya (wife Lacresha)

"Despite 60 years a Viking fan, I'm only giving em' 10 more. Don't blame the family they have fractured into Bronco, Seahawk, Chief, Cowboy, Panther, Bear, and Packer fans."

Acknowledgments

To be able to live past 80, one has to acknowledge some of the helping hands of assistance throughout this trip. Paul E. Dysart, Sr. would like it to be known that the following people are the helping hands that have been very instrumental in helping him put smiles on many faces during this 80 year journey:

William J. Foster, St Joseph Cathedral, Dell Rapids, SD

Bud Stevens, basketball brother in the

US Army, KMAG, Wonju Korea - Asheville, NC

Larry Thomas, Roommate - Minot, ND

Loren Simkins, roomie - Winner, SD

Robin & Gary Gartzki - Watertown, SD

Jim Grotejohn, Business Supt. - Renner, SD

Cork, Butch, John Runge an their families - Sioux Falls, SD

Lulu Waletzki, Carolyn & Peter Dintwe-Lobatse and

Gaborone Botswana

Dr. Kalda, Dr. Bowtie Bradley, Dr. Schechter, Betty Holst and the entire staff at the Sioux Falls, South Dakota Veterans Hospital

Msgr. John McEneaney, St. Joseph Cathedral, Sioux Falls, SD

Dave Munson, Mayor of Sioux Falls, SD

South Dakota US Representative/Senators

Tom Daschle and Tim Johnson

Lloyd Jackson, Phoenix, AZ

Wendell Shaw, Sioux Falls, SD

Claude Fraiser, Des Moines, IA

Made in the USA
Monee, IL
29 April 2022